KS3 Maths Progress

Confidence • Fluency • Problem-solving • Progression

δ ONE

Progression Workbook

Includes videos linked from QR codes!

ALWAYS LEARNING

PEARSON

Contents

Published by Pearson Education Limited, Edinburgh Gate, Harlow, Essex, CM20 2JE.

www.pearsonschoolsandfecolleges.co.uk

Text © Pearson Education Limited 2014
Edited by Project One Publishing Solutions and Elektra Media Ltd
Typeset by Elektra Media Ltd
Original illustrations © Pearson Education Limited 2014
Cover illustration by Robert Samuel Hanson

The right of Greg Byrd to be identified as the author of this work has been asserted by him in accordance with the Copyright, Designs and Patents Act 1988.

First published 2014

24
16

British Library Cataloguing in Publication Data
A catalogue record for this book is available from the British Library.

ISBN 978 1 447 97110 8

Printed and bound by CPI Group (UK) Ltd, Croydon, CR0 4YY

We are grateful to the following for permission to reproduce copyright material:
Northern Ireland homeless and housing data (p9), Department for Social Development Northern Ireland licensed under the Open Government License v.2.0.

Every effort has been made to contact copyright holders of material reproduced in this book. Any omissions will be rectified in subsequent printings if notice is given to the publishers.

Pearson Education Limited is not responsible for the content of any external internet sites. It is essential for tutors to preview each website before using it in class so as to ensure that the URL is still accurate, relevant and appropriate. We suggest that tutors bookmark useful websites and consider enabling students to access them through the school/college intranet.

1 Mahoud and Fahid complete record sheets for their monthly mp3 and mp4 downloads.

> Mahoud: mp3 17 mp4 12
> Fahid: mp3 34 mp4 8

A two-way table splits data into groups in rows across the table and in columns down the table. You can calculate the totals across and down.

a Write Mahoud's data in the top row of the two-way table. Work out the total.

b Write Fahid's data in the second row.

c Work out the total of each column.

d Add the row totals together.
Check by adding the column totals together.

	mp3	mp4	Total
Mahoud	17	12	
Fahid			
Total			

2 The frequency table shows the numbers of pets owned by students in David's and Sian's classes.

	Dogs	Cats	Fish	Insects	Other
David's class	11	9	12	2	7
Sian's class	8	5	2	10	12

a Complete the dual bar chart to display the data.

A **dual bar chart** compares two sets of data.

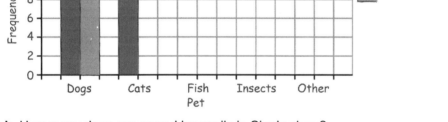

b How many dogs are owned by pupils in Sian's class? _____

c Which type of pet is most popular in David's class? _____

d Whose class has the most pets? _____

Worked example

3 Girls from three different schools were asked which sport they would prefer for their interschool charity sports competition. The two-way table shows the results.

a Complete the compound bar chart.

b How many girls at Greys answered the questionnaire? _____

c Which sport is likely to be played in the competition? Explain.

	Tennis	Football	Hockey	Netball
St Lull	5	30	10	20
Greys	5	10	10	15
Nobel	20	20	10	5

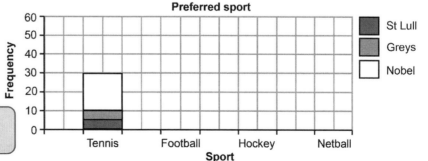

A compound bar chart combines different sets of data in one bar.

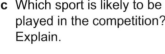

CHECK Tick each box as your **confidence** in this topic improves.

Need extra help? Go to page 7 and tick the box next to Q3. Then have a go at it once you've finished 1.1–1.6.

1

1 Two bird watchers compared notes on the numbers of stonechats they saw last week.

Gill 4, 0, 7, 6, 0, 0, 1

John 3, 1, 3, 2, 3, 2, 1

a Work out the range for

i Gill 7 – 0 = 7   **ii** John. ....

b Whose data is more consistent? ....

> The closer the results are to one another, the more *consistent* they are. The smaller the range, the more consistent the values.

2 The table shows the number of children in each family for Gabbie's class. Work out the mean.

$\text{Mean} = \dfrac{\text{Total number of children}}{\text{Total frequency}}$

$= \dfrac{......}{30} = ...$

Number of children	Frequency	Total number of children
1	15	1 × 15 = 15
2	4	2 × 4 = ...
3	7	
4	4	
Total	30	

> Add a column to work out the total number of children.

> Work out the total frequency and the total number of children.

3 The table shows the numbers of stars given in reviews for a type of skateboard. Work out the mean.

Stars	Frequency
1	12
2	17
3	53
4	18

> **Worked example**
>

4 STEM In biology, Maddi measured the heights of two different types of tomato plants. She used the data to work out the statistics in the table. Write two sentences comparing the heights of the two types of tomato plants.

	Range	Mean
Type A	17 cm	84 cm
Type B	21 cm	76 cm

> **Literacy hint**
> A **statistic** is a way of describing a set of data. Averages (mode, median and mean) and the range are statistics.

5 Here are the weekly amounts of pocket money for a group of students.

£5, £7, £10, £10, £3, £11, £8, £50, £5, £10

a Which amount is an extreme value? ....

b Work out the mean, median and mode.

> An **extreme value** is one that is much bigger or smaller than the other values.

c Which average best describes their weekly pocket money? Explain.

> The **average** gives a typical value for a set of data. The mode, median and mean are different ways of describing the average.

CHECK Tick each box as your **confidence** in this topic improves.

Need extra help? Go to page 7 and tick the boxes next to Q1 and 2. Then have a go at them once you've finished 1.1–1.6.

1.3 Grouped data

1 Real / STEM Every weekend, Ros picks up rubbish from her local beach.
The table shows the numbers of plastic items collected.
Complete the sentences.

Plastic items	Frequency
100–199	2
200–299	18
300–399	25
400–499	7

a Between 200 and 299 items were collected on .... weekends.

b Between 300 and 399 items were collected on .... weekends.

c The modal class is ....

> The **modal class** is the one with the highest frequency.

2 Write whether each set of data is discrete or continuous.

a The numbers of students in classrooms. ....

b The heights of students. ....

c The masses of students. ....

d Students' pocket money amounts. ....

> **Discrete data** can only take particular values. For example, dress sizes can only be even numbers. For discrete data you can use groups like 1–10, 11–20 …
> **Continuous data** is measured and can take any value. For example, length, mass and capacity. For continuous data there are no gaps between the groups.

3 Adam measured the arm spans, s cm, of the students in his class.

~~120 cm~~, 133 cm, 135 cm, 140 cm, ~~129 cm~~,

155 cm, 140 cm, 134 cm, 137 cm, 141 cm,

145 cm, 130 cm, 139 cm, 135 cm, 142 cm

> Continuous data is grouped into continuous **class intervals**.
> The class interval 140 cm $\leq h <$ 150 cm includes all heights h between 140 cm and 150 cm.
> The $\leq$ symbol means that 140 cm is included.
> The $<$ symbol means that 150 cm is not included.
> The width of this class is 10 cm.

a Complete the grouped frequency table for the data. Make the classes have equal widths.

Arm span, s (cm)	Frequency
$120 \leq s < 130$	2
$130 \leq s <$	
.... $\leq s <$	
.... $\leq s <$	

b What is the modal class? --------------------------------------

4 a Use your grouped frequency table from Q3 to complete the frequency diagram.

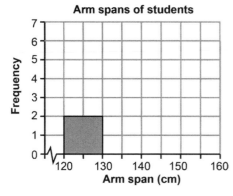

For continuous data, there are no spaces between the bars.

b How many students have an arm span of at least 140 cm? ....

CHECK Tick each box as your **confidence** in this topic improves.

Need extra help? Go to page 8 and tick the box next to Q5. Then have a go at it once you've finished 1.1–1.6.

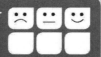

1 Modelling The table shows the maximum daily temperatures in Glasgow for one week.

Day	Mon	Tue	Wed	Thu	Fri	Sat	Sun
Temperature (°C)	24	25	28	28	27	27	23

When a line graph shows changes over time, put time on the horizontal axis.

a Plot the points using crosses. Join the points with a ruler.

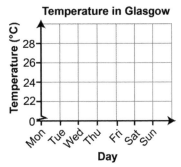

The zig-zag shows there's a break in the axis scale.

Worked example

b Dalgleish says this is not a good model for predicting the temperature for the next few months. Explain why he is correct.

'Explain' means write a sentence: *This is not a good model because*

2 Two pans of water are heated. Pan B contains 250 m*l* more water than pan A. The graph shows the recorded temperatures.

a What was the recorded temperature in pan A after 60 seconds? ....

b What was the difference in temperature between the two pans after 120 seconds? ....

c Write a sentence to compare the times taken by the two pans to reach 100 °C.

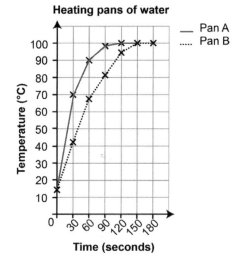

Heating pans of water

— Pan A
..... Pan B

3 Reasoning Explain why each of these graphs is misleading.

a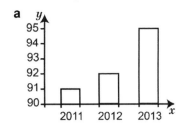

b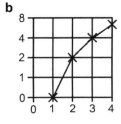

c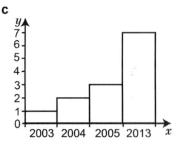

a ....

b ....

c ....

1 Some students were asked whether global climate change was actually happening.
The table shows the students' replies.
Draw a pie chart to show this data.

Reply	Frequency	Angle
Yes	18	
No	4	
Unsure	14	

Number of students = 18 + 4 + 14 = 36

÷ 36 (36 students are 360°) ÷ 36
(1 student is 10°)

Angle for 'Yes':

× 18 (1 student is 10°) × 18
(18 students are 180°)

Angle for 'No' = 4 × .... = ... °

Angle for 'Unsure' = ... °

Check: 180° + ... ° + ... ° = 360° ✓

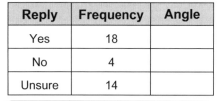

1 Work out the total frequency.
2 Work out the angle for one student.
3 Work out the angle for each reply.
4 Check the angles add up to 360°.

A pie chart is a circle divided into slices called sectors.
The whole circle represents a set of data.
Each sector represents a fraction of the data.

Students' replies

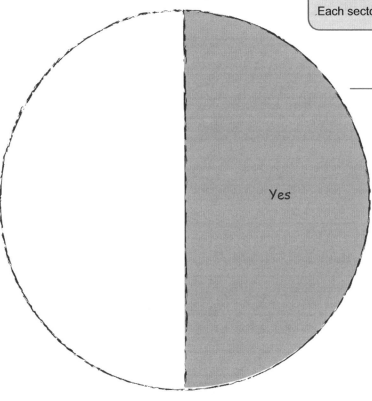

Yes

Draw the pie chart.
Draw in a radius.
Then use a protractor to draw the angles.
Label each sector or make a key
(you do not have to label the angles).
Give your pie chart a title.

Worked example

2 Pablo needs to draw a pie chart for each of these tables of results.
Work out the angles for Pablo.

a

Pet	Frequency	Angle
Cat	6	
Dog	10	
Other	2	

b

Car	Percentage	Angle
BMW	25%	
Ford	25%	
Seat	40%	
Lotus	10%	

CHECK Tick each box as your **confidence** in this topic improves.

Need extra help? Go to page 7 and tick the box next to Q4. Then have a go at it once you've finished 1.1–1.6.

1 STEM / Reasoning The table shows the blood alcohol concentration (BAC) of 12 volunteers, in milligrams per litre, and their reaction time to do a simple task.

BAC (mg/l)	6	50	70	42	2	60	50	28	40	30	14	76
Time (s)	1.4	2.0	5.2	4.1	1.7	4.0	4.5	3.0	3.5	3.5	2.0	5.1

a Draw a scatter graph to show this data.

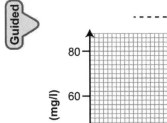

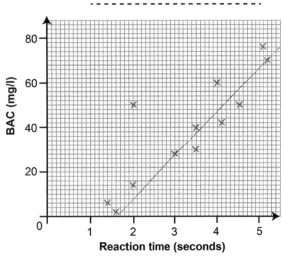

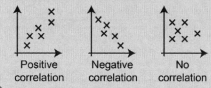

A **scatter graph** shows two sets of data on the same graph. The shape of a scatter graph shows if there is a relationship or **correlation** between two sets of data.

Positive correlation   Negative correlation   No correlation

Draw a line from 4.0 seconds to the line of best fit. Draw a line across and read off the BAC.

A line of best fit shows the relationship between two sets of data.
There should be about the same number of crosses on each side of the line.
There may also be crosses on the line. A good line here would be from (1.6,0) to (5.4,76).

b Describe the correlation shown by the scatter graph.

c Write down the BAC of the person who

took 4 seconds. ....

d Kabali thinks one point has been plotted incorrectly. Which point do you think this is? Explain.

e Draw a line of best fit.

f Use your line of best fit to estimate the BAC of

someone who takes 4 seconds. ....

2 STEM / Real The table shows the width and length of 7 razor clam shells.

Width (cm)	1.3	2.1	2.3	2.8	3.0	3.4	3.6
Length (cm)	6.0	9.6	10.2	12.8	13.4	15.0	16.2

a Draw a scatter graph for this data.

b Draw a line of best fit on your scatter graph.

c Use your line of best fit to estimate

   i the length of a 2.5 cm wide shell ....

   ii the width of a 12 cm long shell. ....

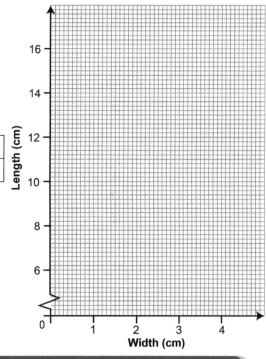

Size of razor clams

CHECK Tick each box as your **confidence** in this topic improves.

Need extra help? Go to page 8 and tick the box next to Q7. Then have a go at it once you've finished 1.1–1.6.

1 Strengthen

Averages and range

1 Chris recorded the number of species of birds visiting a bird table each hour one Saturday morning: 6, 2, 2, 0, 4

   a Work out **i** the range 6 – .... = ...   **ii** the mean. $\dfrac{6+2+2+0+4}{5}$ = ...

   b The numbers for Sunday morning were: 3, 2, 3, 2, 2

     Work out **i** the range ....   **ii** the mean. ....

2 Dana asked her friends how many TVs were in their house.

   a Complete her frequency table.

   b How many TVs are there in total? ....

   c How many friends did Dana ask?

     total frequency = ...

   d Work out the mean number of TVs.

     mean = total TVs ÷ total frequency = ...

TVs	Frequency	Total TVs
1	5	5 × 1 = 5
2	8	
3	5	
4	6	
Total		

> 5 friends
> × 1 TV each
> = 5 TVs

Charts and tables

3 Students from classes 7A and 7B were asked if they preferred going to a theme park, the cinema or an ice rink.
The table and the two bar charts show the same data.

	7A	7B
Park		
Cinema		
Rink	12	10

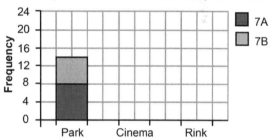

Compound bar chart of students' preferences

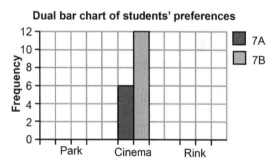

Dual bar chart of students' preferences

   a Use the compound bar chart to work out the number of students who chose theme park.

   b Use the dual bar chart to work out the number of students who chose the cinema.

   c Use the two way table to complete the two bar charts.

4 The table shows the favourite yoghurt flavours of 15 students.

Flavour	Frequency	Sector angle
Vanilla	5	
Strawberry	2	
Lemon	1	
Toffee	7	

Yoghurt flavour preference

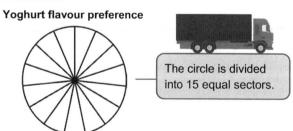

> The circle is divided into 15 equal sectors.

   a Work out the angle of one sector. 360° ÷ 15 = ...°

   b How many sectors would you shade for lemon flavour? ....

   c How many sectors would you shade for strawberry flavour? ....

   d Complete the column of sector angles. Check that they add up to 360°.

   e Complete the pie chart to show the favourite yoghurt flavours.

5 Joe has drawn a tally chart to show the times taken by 20 students to complete a puzzle.

a He must add one more tally. The time is 20 seconds. Add this data to the tally chart.

b Complete the frequency column.

c Which is the modal class? _____

d Complete the frequency diagram to show this data.

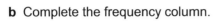

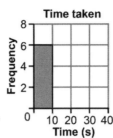

Time, t (s)	Tally	Frequency
$0 \leq t < 10$	卌 I	
$10 \leq t < 20$	卌 III	
$20 \leq t < 30$	IIII	
$30 \leq t < 40$	I	

Line graphs, scatter graphs and correlation

6 Hank recorded his best long jumps so far this year. He drew two graphs to show his results.

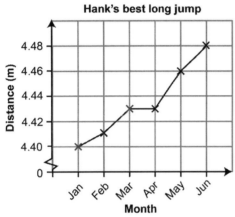

Make sure you give reasons why the first graph makes Hank look better.

Which graph makes Hank look better? Why?

The first graph because _____

7 In an experiment, students were allowed different amounts of time to study for a test. The table shows the number of mistakes they each made.

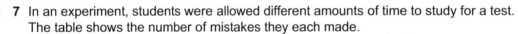

Mistakes	52	47	38	41	35	29	11	19	10	6
Time (hours)	1	1	1.5	2	2	2.5	3	3	3.5	4

Positive correlation: looking from the vertical axis, the points go 'uphill': the values are increasing.
Negative correlation: looking from the vertical axis, the points go 'downhill': the values are decreasing.
No correlation: the points are not close to a straight line, uphill or downhill.

a Draw a scatter graph for the data on the grid.

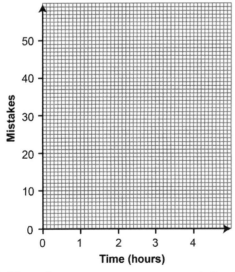

Worked example

b There is a _____ correlation between the number of mistakes made and studying time.

c Draw a straight line of best fit.

d Use your line of best fit to estimate the number of mistakes made after 2 hours of study. _____

1 Problem-solving Aaron and Bryony each surveyed students. They asked them, 'Will all cars be electric in 2050?'. The compound bar chart shows their results.

a Who got the greater percentage of 'Unsure'? ....

b What percentage of Aaron's replies were 'No'? ....

c Aaron asked 200 students. Bryony asked 10 students.

   How many of Aaron's replies were 'Unsure'? ....

d Complete the two-way table to show the numbers of replies from the two surveys.

	Unsure	No	Yes
Aaron			
Bryony			

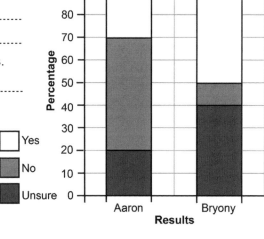

Electric cars by 2050?

Yes / No / Unsure

2 Real / Reasoning The line graph shows the number of homeless people and the total number of houses in Northern Ireland.

a How many homeless people

   were there in 2008? ....

b How many houses were there

   in 2005? ....

c A newspaper wrote this with the graph: 'Before 2007 the number of homeless was greater than the total number of houses available.'
   Explain why the quote is wrong.

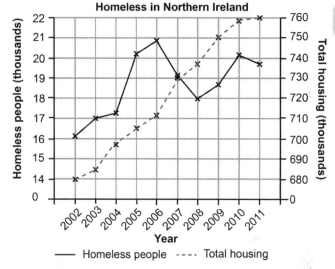

Homeless in Northern Ireland

—— Homeless people ---- Total housing

Source: Department for Social Development Northern Ireland

3 a Here are the masses, in kg, of the first six runners to cross the line in a 100 m final.

   94, 76, 83, 75, 82, 74

   i What is their median mass? ....

   ii Work out the range. ....

   iii Calculate their mean mass. ....

b The table shows some statistics about the masses of the first six runners in the 1500 m final. Write two sentences comparing the masses of the two sets of runners.

Mean	Median	Range
62.5	61	13

4 The table shows the masses, m kg, of a class of Year 7 students.

a Complete the table.

b How many boys have a mass

   of at least 35 kg? ....

c Compare the average masses of the boys and the girls.

	$25 \leq m < 35$	$35 \leq m < 45$	$45 \leq m < 55$	Total
Boys	7	6	3	
Girls	3	7	4	
Total				

5 a The masses of five mice are 30 g, 29 g, 30 g, 32 g and 33 g.
Use an assumed mean of 30 g to calculate the mean mass.

The **assumed mean** is a sensible
estimate for the mean.

$$30 \quad 29 \quad 30 \quad 32 \quad 33$$

Differences from 30:　　0　-1　0　+2　+3 = 4

Mean of differences =　　4 ÷ 5 = 0.8

The values are all close to 30 g,
so the assumed mean is 30 g.
Work out the differences from 30.

Mean = assumed mean + mean of differences = 30 + 0.8 = 30.8 g

b The masses of five rats are 162 g, 168 g, 154 g, 159 g and 161 g.
Use an assumed mean to calculate the mean mass.

What would be
a sensible
assumed mean
for these data?

Worked example

6 Problem-solving Alex and six friends noted how many sit-ups
and press-ups they could each do.

Student	Alex	Cal	Eli	Gus	Ian	Pat	Ray
Sit-ups	18	15	22	19	28	25	17
Press-ups	10	4	12	9	19	14	8

a Draw a suitable graph to display the data.

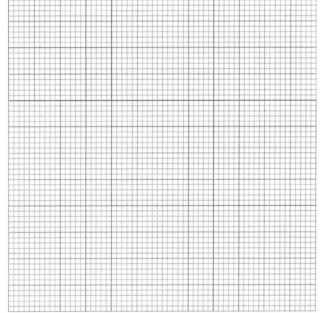

b Tom can do 24 sit-ups.
Use your graph to estimate the number of press-ups he could do. ....

Draw a line of best
fit and use it to
make an estimate.

Alex kept a record of the number of sit-ups he did per week.

c Draw a pie chart to show his data.

Sit-ups, s	Frequency
$100 \le s < 120$	6
$120 \le s < 140$	12
$140 \le s < 160$	4
$160 \le s < 180$	2

The pie chart will have 4 sectors.
Work out the total frequency first.

d What is the modal class for Alex's number of sit-ups? ....

e Complete this sentence.

For 25% of the weeks Alex did at least .... sit-ups per week.

1 Unit test

> **PROGRESS BAR** Colour in the progress bar as you get questions correct.
> Then fill in the progression chart on pages 107-109.

1 The table shows the numbers of items hand-painted by Fin and Paj on Monday.

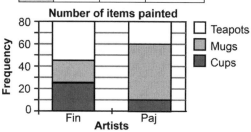

	Cups	Mugs	Teapots
Fin	20	40	10
Paj	50	10	20

a How many items did Fin paint on Monday? ....

b How many mugs were painted altogether? ....

c How many items were painted altogether? ....

d The compound bar chart shows the numbers of items hand-painted by Fin and Paj on Friday. How many mugs were painted on both days altogether?

2 Betty recorded the number of 'bullseyes' she hit at archery practice each week.

7, 7, 4, 10, 6, 10, 39, 13, 9, 7

Which average should she use to describe the data? Explain your answer.

3 The table shows the distances travelled by a lorry driver.

Distance (miles)	152	201	350	279	501	388	412	230	137	255

Work out the mean distance travelled.

4 Here are the times taken, in seconds, for 15 students to send a text.

13, 22, 23, 9, 46, 30, 18, 5, 13, 29, 13, 9, 32, 26, 25

a Complete the tally chart for the data.

b What is the modal class?

Time, t (s)	Tally	Frequency
$0 \le t < 10$		
$10 \le t < 20$		
$20 \le t < 30$		
$30 \le t < 40$		
$40 \le t < 50$		

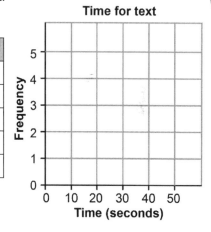

c Complete the frequency diagram for the data.

5 The table shows the pulse and breathing rates (per minute) of ten people during different activities.

Pulses per minute	62	68	72	75	85	84	90	88	96
Breaths per minute	17	19	21	21	25	27	29	29	31

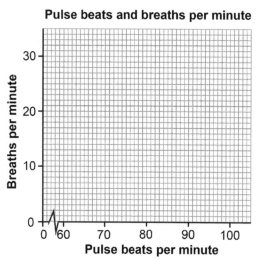

a Draw a scatter graph for the data using these axes.

b Describe the correlation between breathing rate and pulse rate. ....

c Draw a line of best fit.

d Val has a pulse rate of 80 per minute.

Estimate her breathing rate. ....

2.1 Factors, primes and multiples

1 Here is a list of numbers.

1, 2, 3, 4, 5, 6, 7, 8, 9, 10, 11, 12, 13, 14,

15, 16, 17, 18, 19, 20, 21, 22, 23, 24, 25

Circle the prime numbers.

> A **prime number** has exactly two factors: 1 and itself.

Guided

2 a Write down all the factors of

  i 12 1 × 12 = 12, 2 × 6 = 12, 3 × 4 = 12. Factors are 1, 2, 3, 4, 6, 12

  ii 18 1 × 18, 2 × _____

  iii 25 _____

b Write down all of the prime factors of each number in part **a**.

  i 2, 3

  ii _____

  iii _____

> A **prime factor** is a factor of a number that is also a prime number.

3 **Problem-solving** Simon finds all the factors of a number. This is his list.

1, 2, 3, 4, ____ , ____ , 8, 10, 12, ____ , ____ , 20, 24, ____ , ____ , 48, ____ , 80, 120, 240

What are the missing numbers?

4 a Write down all the factors of 6. _____

  b Write down all the factors of 15. _____

  c Write down the common factors of 6 and 15. _____

  d What is the **highest common factor** (HCF) of 6 and 15? _____

  e Find the HCF of each of these pairs of numbers.

    i 8 and 20 _____

    ii 9 and 27 _____

> The **highest common factor (HCF)** of two numbers is the largest number that is a factor of both numbers.

Worked example

5 a List the first 8 multiples of 4. _____

  b List the first 8 multiples of 8. _____

  c Write down the common multiples of 4 and 8

    that are in both lists. _____

  d What is the **lowest common multiple** (LCM) of 4 and 8? _____

> The **lowest common multiple (LCM)** of two numbers is the smallest number that is a multiple of both numbers.

6 **STEM** The diagram shows two cogs.
The larger cog has 10 teeth and the smaller cog has 6 teeth.
The cogs start to turn with the black dots next to each other.
What is the smallest number of turns each cog must make
before the black dots are next to each other again?

CHECK Tick each box as your **confidence** in this topic improves.

Need extra help? Go to page 18 and tick the boxes next to Q1–3. Then have a go at them once you've finished 2.1–2.6.

2.2 Using negative numbers

1 Use this number line to work out

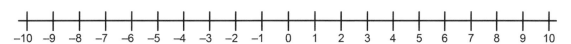

$$-10 \quad -9 \quad -8 \quad -7 \quad -6 \quad -5 \quad -4 \quad -3 \quad -2 \quad -1 \quad 0 \quad 1 \quad 2 \quad 3 \quad 4 \quad 5 \quad 6 \quad 7 \quad 8 \quad 9 \quad 10$$

a $9 - 11$ .... **b** $-6 + 10$ ....

c $-4 - 5$ .... **d** $-9 + 3$ ....

> Numbers without a sign in front of them are positive. So $4 - 3$ is $+4 - +3$.

2 a Complete these patterns.

> **i** $4 + 3 = 7$ **ii** $4 - 3 = 1$
>
> $4 + 2 = 6$ $4 - 2 = 2$
>
> $4 + 1 =$ .... $4 - 1 =$ ....
>
> $4 + 0 =$ .... $4 - 0 =$ ....
>
> $4 + -1 =$ .... $4 - -1 =$ ....
>
> $4 + -2 =$ .... $4 - -2 =$ ....

b Reasoning Which sign, + or −, is missing from each statement?

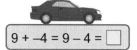

$9 + -4 = 9 - 4 = \boxed{}$

> **i** $4 + -2$ is the same as 4 ..... 2.
>
> **ii** $4 - -2$ is the same as 4 ..... 2.

c Complete these rules.

replace $+ +$ with $+$, replace $+ -$ with $-$, replace $- +$ with ...., replace $- -$ with ....

3 Work out

a $9 + -4$ .... **b** $-3 + 7$ .... **c** $-15 + -2$ .... **d** $-2 - -3$ ....

4 a Complete these patterns.

> **i** $5 \times 2 = 10$ **ii** $-5 \times 2 = -10$
>
> $5 \times 1 = 5$ $-5 \times 1 =$ ....
>
> $5 \times 0 =$ .... $-5 \times 0 =$ ....
>
> $5 \times -1 =$ .... $-5 \times -1 =$ ....
>
> $5 \times -2 =$ .... $-5 \times -2 =$ ....

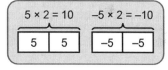

$5 \times 2 = 10$ $-5 \times 2 = -10$

| 5 | 5 | | −5 | −5 |

b Complete these rules.

positive $\times$ positive $=$ positive, positive $\times$ negative $=$ ....

negative $\times$ positive $=$ ...., negative $\times$ negative $=$ ....

5 Work out

a 5×-5 .... **b** -4×3 .... **c** -6×-6 .... **d** $-2 \times -3 \times -5$ ....

6 Work out

a $35 \div -5$ ....

b $-40 \div 4$ ....

c $-18 \div -6$ ....

> Division is the inverse of multiplication. Multiplication is the inverse of division.
> $+ \div + = +$ $+ \div - = -$
> $- \div + = -$, $- \div - = +$

CHECK   Tick each box as your **confidence** in this topic improves.

Need extra help? Go to page 18 and tick the boxes next to Q5 and 6. Then have a go at them once you've finished 2.1–2.6.

Guided

1 a Estimate the answer to each of these by rounding to the nearest 10.

    i $19 \times 32 \approx 20 \times$ .... $=$ ....

    ii 38×73 ....

b Work out the accurate answers to the calculations in part **a**.
Use your estimates to check your answers.

> **Literacy hint**
> In maths, estimation means using rounded values to do the calculation. $\approx$ means 'is approximately equal to'.

2 Work out

    a 3×56 ....

    b 6×28 ....

    c 12×14 ....

    d Reasoning Write down another multiplication which gives the same answer as **a**, **b** and **c**.

3 Problem-solving / Reasoning In these number wheels, opposite numbers multiply to give the number in the middle. Complete the number wheels.

a

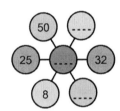

b

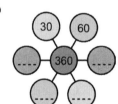

Guided

4 Using long division, work out $523 \div 11$.

Estimate: $523 \div 11 \approx 520 \div 10 = 52$

```
        4 ....
   11 | 5  2  3
    -  4  4          4 × 11 = 44
       8  3
    -     7  7       7 × 11 = 77
             6
```

> $4 \times 11 = 44$. So 11 goes into 52 4 times. $3 - 0 = 3$, so bring down 3.

> Try multiplying 11 by different numbers to get close to 83. $7 \times 11 = 77$

> 6 is less than 11, so the remainder is 6.

$523 \div 11 =$ ..... remainder .....   Check: ..... remainder ..... is close to $52 \checkmark$

5 Work out

    a $336 \div 12$ **b** $485 \div 15$ **c** $975 \div 51$

> Estimate first.
> Use your estimate to check your answer.

Worked example

CHECK   Tick each box as your **confidence** in this topic improves.

Need extra help? Go to page 18 and tick the box next to Q4. Then have a go at it once you've finished 2.1–2.6.

2.4 Squares and square roots

1 a Complete this table showing all the square numbers from 1 to 15.

1^2	2^2	3^2	4^2	5^2	6^2	7^2	8^2	9^2	10^2	11^2	12^2	13^2	14^2	15^2
1	4													

b Use your table in part **a** to write down the answers to these.

i $\sqrt{9}$ .... **ii** $\sqrt{49}$ .... **iii** $\sqrt{144}$ ....

> To find the square of a number you multiply it by itself.
> $3^2 = 3 \times 3 = 9$
> 3^2 means '3 squared'.

2 a Complete these.

i $5 \times 5 = 25$

$-5 \times -5 = 25$

so, $\sqrt{25} = 5$ or ....

ii $10 \times 10 =$ ....

$-10 \times -10 =$ ....

so, $\sqrt{100} =$ .... or ....

> The inverse of square is **square root**.
> $3^2 = 3 \times 3 = 9$, so the square root of 9 is
> $\sqrt{9} = 3$

b Write down both answers to each of these.

i $\sqrt{16}$ 4 or –4 **ii** $\sqrt{225}$ .... **iii** $\sqrt{4}$ ....

3 Reasoning A square has area 64 cm^2.
Nick says, 'The side length of the square could be 8 cm or –8 cm because the square root of 64 is 8 or –8.'
Tammy says, 'The side length of the square can only be 8 cm.'
Who is correct? Explain your answer.

4 Check each of these calculations is correct by using the inverse operation.

a $19^2 = 361$ **b** $5.5^2 = 30.25$ **c** $\sqrt{24.01} = 4.9$

> **a** Work out $\sqrt{361}$.
> **c** Work out 4.9^2.

5 a Work out an estimate for these square roots.

i $\sqrt{28}$ $\sqrt{25} = 5$, $\sqrt{36} = 6$. So $\sqrt{28}$ lies between 5 and 6. Estimate is 5.3

ii $\sqrt{47}$

iii $\sqrt{110}$ ....

> Use your table from Q1 to help you.
> 28 is closer to 25 than 36, so estimate a bit less than 5.5.

b Check your estimates by working out the accurate square roots on a calculator.

6 Work out

a 3^2 .... **b** 30^2 ....

c 300^2 .... **d** 0.3^2 ....

7 Work out

a $\sqrt{400}$ .... **b** $\sqrt{4} \times \sqrt{100}$ ....

c $\sqrt{900}$ .... **d** $\sqrt{9} \times \sqrt{100}$ ....

e $\sqrt{8100}$ .... **f** $\sqrt{3969}$ ....

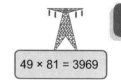

$49 \times 81 = 3969$

CHECK Tick each box as your **confidence** in this topic improves.

Need extra help? Go to page 19 and tick the boxes next to Q8, 9 and 11. Then have a go at the once you've finished 2.1–2.6.

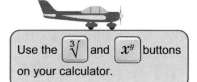

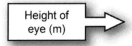

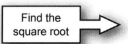

1 Complete this table showing commonly used cube numbers.

1^3	2^3	3^3	4^3	5^3	6^3	10^3
1	8				216	

> To find the cube of a number, multiply it by itself and then multiply by the number again.
> $2^3 = 2 \times 2 \times 2 = 8$
> 2^3 means '2 cubed' or '2 to the power 3'.
> 3 is the power.

2 Use your table in Q1 to write down the answers to these.

a $\sqrt[3]{8}$ ....

b $\sqrt[3]{216}$ ....

c $\sqrt[3]{64}$ ....

d $\sqrt[3]{-27}$ ....

> The inverse of cube is **cube root**.
> $2^3 = 8$, so the cube root of 8 is $\sqrt[3]{8} = 2$.

> **d** $\square \times \square \times \square = 27$
> $\square \times \square \times \square = -27$

3 Work out

a $5^2 + 5 = 25 + 5 =$ ....

b $2 \times 4^2 + 1 = 32 + 1$ ....

c $\dfrac{8^2}{2}$ ....

d $\dfrac{\sqrt{81}}{3} + 3 \times 9$ ....

> Squares, cubes, square roots are indices or powers.
> The priority of operations is
> • Brackets
> • Indices or Powers
> • Multiplication and Division
> • Addition and Subtraction

4 Work out

a $2^3 \times 5$ ....

b 10×3^3 ....

c $\dfrac{5^3}{25}$ ....

d $5 \times \sqrt[3]{1000}$ ....

e $\dfrac{50}{\sqrt[3]{125}}$ ....

f $6^2 - 3^3$ ....

g $2 \times \sqrt[3]{64} + 2$ ....

h $\dfrac{4^3}{\sqrt[3]{64}} - \dfrac{4^2}{\sqrt{64}}$ ....

5 Use a calculator to work out

a $8^3 - 12$ ....

b $3 \times 21^2 - 323$ ....

c $31 \times 12^2 - 0.5 \times 12^3$ ....

d $5 \times \sqrt[3]{512} + 10$ ....

e $\dfrac{\sqrt[3]{2744}}{\sqrt{784}} + 4.5$ ....

Use the $\sqrt[3]{}$ and x^y buttons on your calculator.

6 STEM / Modelling   You can estimate the distance to the horizon using this flowchart.

Height of eye (m)	→	Multiply by 13	→	Find the square root	→	Distance (km)

Work out the distance to the horizon when it is seen from a height of

a 1.5 m ....

b 10 m ....

c 20 m. ....

7 Problem-solving $512 = 8 \times 64$
Use this fact to work out $\sqrt[3]{512}$.

> $512 = 8 \times 64$,
> so $\sqrt[3]{512} = \sqrt[3]{8} \times \sqrt[3]{64}$

CHECK   Tick each box as your **confidence** in this topic improves.

Need extra help? Go to page 19 and tick the boxes next to Q8 and 10. Then have a go at them once you've finished 2.1–2.6.

1 a Estimate the answer to each calculation.

i $51 + 6.8 \times 32 \approx 50 + 7 \times$ .... = ...

ii $25 \times 62 - 13 \times 76$ ....

iii $\frac{88.4}{29.02} + 5.4 \times 8.1$ ....

iv $\frac{83}{38.2} \times 6.3 + 9.1$ ....

> Round numbers less than 10 to the nearest whole number. Round larger numbers to the nearest 10.

b Use a calculator to work out the accurate answers to the calculations in part **a**.

i .... **ii** .... **iii** .... **iv** ....

Use your estimates to check your answers.

2 Work out

a $(15 - 5)^2 = 10^2 =$ ....

b $(2 + 2 \times 2)^2 = (2 + 4)^2 =$ .... $^2 =$ ....

c $\left(\frac{24}{6} + 5\right)^2$ ....

d $\sqrt{40 - 4} = \sqrt{36} =$ ....

e $(-4)^3 = -4 \times -4 \times$ .... = ...

f $\sqrt{120 + 12 \times 2}$ ....

> The priority of operations is
> • Brackets
> • Indices or Powers
> • Multiplication and Division
> • Addition and Subtraction

3 Work out these calculations.
Check your answers using a calculator.

a $5 \times (\sqrt{64} - 1)$ ....

b $(5^2 - \sqrt{100})^2$ ....

c $9^2 - (14 + \sqrt{49})$ ....

d $(4 \times 6 - 21)^3$ ....

e $4^3 + (3 + 2)^3$ ....

f $3 \times 2^3 + 6$ ....

> Use the (and) buttons on your calculator.

> **Worked example**
>

4 Work out

a $\frac{32 + 8}{6 - 2}$ ....

b $\frac{1 + 7^2}{5}$ ....

c $\frac{5^3 - 5^2}{4 \times 5}$ ....

d $\frac{\sqrt{64}}{4 + 4}$ ....

e $\frac{\sqrt{225} - 3}{3}$ ....

f $\frac{10^2 - 10}{\sqrt[3]{125}}$ ....

> The dividing line of the fraction acts like a bracket.
> $\frac{32 + 8}{6 - 2} = (32 + 8) \div (6 - 2)$

5 a Match each calculation card with the correct answer card.
Check your answers using a calculator.

$\sqrt{1 + 4^2 + 4^3}$ $\sqrt[3]{30 - 3}$ $24 - 9 - \sqrt[3]{64}$ $7 \times (6 - \sqrt[3]{125})$

3   5   7   9   11

b There is one answer card left over. Write a calculation card to go with this answer card.
The calculation must include a cube root or a square root.

CHECK Tick each box as your **confidence** in this topic improves.

Need extra help? Go to page 19 and tick the boxes next to Q7, 12, 13 and 14. Then have a go at them once you've finished 2.1–2.6.

2 Strengthen

Working with numbers

1 a Work out the common factors of 16 and 24.

Factors of 16: 1, 2, 4, 8, 16

Factors of 24: 1, 2, ..., ..., ..., ..., ..., ...

The common factors are 1, 2, ..., ...

b What is the highest common factor of 16 and 24? ....

> Circle the numbers that are the same in both lists.
> These are the common factors.

2 Work out the highest common factor of 18 and 27.

> Follow the same steps as Q1.

3 a Write a list of multiples of 3 that are less than 35.

3, 6, 9, 12, 15, 18, ...

b Write a list of multiples of 5 that are less than 35. ....

c Write down the common multiples of 3 and 5 that are less than 35. ....

d Write down the lowest common multiple of 3 and 5. ....

> Circle the numbers that are the same in both lists.
> These are the common multiples.

4 Work out

a 624 ÷ 12

1 × 12 = 12	4 × 12 = ...	7 × 12 = ...
2 × 12 = 24	5 × 12 = ...	8 × 12 = ...
3 × 12 = ...	6 × 12 = ...	9 × 12 = ...

> Write out the first 9 multiples of 12 to help you.

```
      5 .....
12 | 6 2 4
   - 6 0        5 × 12 = 60
     2 4
   -  2 4       ......... × 12 = 24
        0       There is no remainder.
```

b 286 ÷ 11

$$11 \overline{)286}$$

5 Work out

a 9 − −4 = 9 −(−)4 = 9 (+) 4 = ...

b 8 + −5 = 8(+ −)5 = 8 − 5 = ...

c −6 − −4 ....

d −7 + − 3 ....

> Replace − − with +
> Replace + − with −

6 Work out

> Different signs → negative answer
> Same signs → positive answer

a 5 × −4   5 × 4 = ..., + × − → − answer: − ....

b −30 ÷ −5   30 ÷ 5 = ..., − ÷ − → + answer: ....

c −3 × −7 ....

d −25 ÷ 5 ....

Worked example

7 Estimate the answer to each calculation.

a $\dfrac{38}{5.8}$ ....

b $\dfrac{61}{8.2}$ ....

c $21.6 - \dfrac{11}{3.8}$ ....

> Round the 'bottom' number.
> $5.8 \approx 6$
> Then round the 'top' number to a multiple of 6.

Powers and roots

8 Work out the missing numbers.

> $2^3 \longleftarrow$ index
> The index tells you how many 2s are
> multiplied together. $2^3 = 2 \times 2 \times 2$

a $2^3 = 2 \times 2 \times 2 = $ ....

b $4^3 = $ .... × .... × .... = ...

c .... $^{....} = 5 \times 5 = $ ....   d .... $^{....} = 10 \times $ .... = ...

9 a Complete this number line.

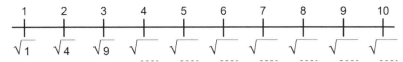

b Use the number line to estimate a value for these square roots.

  i $\sqrt{14}$ ....   **ii** $\sqrt{30}$ ....   **iii** $\sqrt{84}$ ....

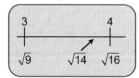

10 Work out these calculations.

a $3 \times 4^2 = 3 \times$ .... × .... $= 3 \times$ .... $=$ ....

b $\dfrac{9}{\sqrt[3]{27}} + 8^2 = \dfrac{9}{....} + $ .... × .... $=$ .... + ... $=$ ....

c $12 + 2^3 = 12 + 2 \times$ .... × .... $= 12 + $ .... $=$ ....

d $\dfrac{10^3}{100}$ ....

> Work out numbers with an index
> before multiplication or division.
> Work out multiplication or division
> before addition or subtraction.

11 $1064 = 64 \times 16$

Use this fact to work out $\sqrt{1024}$.

$\sqrt{1024} = \sqrt{64} \times \sqrt{16} = \square \times \square = \square$

Working with brackets

12 Work out

> Work out the brackets first.

a $(5 \times 4 - 11)^2$ $5 \times 4 - 11 = 20 - 11 = $ ...., answer: ....$^2 =$ ....

b $(21 - 8 \times 2)^3$ ....   c $6 + (13 - \sqrt{100})^2$ ....

13 Work out

a $\sqrt{32 + 32} = \sqrt{64} = $ ....   b $\sqrt{4^2 + 9}$ ....

> Work out the calculation
> under the square root first.

14 Work out

> Calculate the top and
> bottom of the fraction first.

a $\dfrac{44 + 6}{22 + 3} = \dfrac{.....}{.....} = $ ....   b $\dfrac{34 - 3^2}{5}$ ....

c $\dfrac{8 + 24}{4^2}$ ....   d $\dfrac{10^2 - 20}{\sqrt{16}}$ ....   e $\dfrac{\sqrt[3]{27} + 5}{2^2}$ ....

1 Problem-solving / Finance Ross buys a new car that costs £10 440.
He pays a deposit of £3000.
He then pays the remaining amount in 24 equal monthly instalments.
How much does Ross pay each month?

Guided

£10 440 – £3000 = ...

Each monthly payment: .... ÷ 24   24⟌.........

> A **deposit** is the amount you
> pay on the day you buy an item.
> An **instalment** is the amount
> you pay on a regular basis,
> e.g. monthly.

2 Write these numbers in ascending order.

3^3, 5^2, 5^3, 11^2 ....

> **Literacy hint**
> Numbers in **ascending** order
> go from smallest to largest.

3 a Write down all the factors of

i   27 ....

ii 36 ....

iii 45 ....

b Write down the HCF of 27, 36 and 45. ....

4 a Write down the first 10 multiples of

i   4 ....

ii 5 ....

iii 8 ....

b Write down the LCM of 4, 5 and 8. ....

5 Problem-solving Santa turns on three sets of flashing Christmas lights at the same time.
One set flashes every 2 seconds, one set every 3 seconds and the third set every 5 seconds.
How long after they are first turned on do they next flash together at
the same time?

> **Strategy hint**
> Write out the first 10
> multiples of 2, 3 and 5.

6 Problem-solving / Reasoning The area of a square is 40 cm².
Ghida says, 'I think the side length of the square is about 5.9 cm.'
Without working out the side length, explain how you know there is a better estimate.

7 STEM Tony tests electrical appliances to make sure they are safe. He uses the rule

$$\text{current} = \sqrt{\frac{\text{power}}{\text{resistance}}}$$

Current is measured in amperes, A. Power is measured in watts, W.
Resistance is measured in ohms, Ω.
Work out the current when power = 1500 W and resistance = 15 Ω.

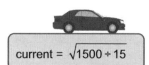

> current = $\sqrt{1500 \div 15}$

8 Give both possible answers to the calculation $\sqrt{3 \times 7 + 4}$.

> $\sqrt{100}$ = 10 or –10

9 Work out

a $(-5)^2 = -5 \times -5 = $ ....

b $(8 - 3 \times 5)^2$ ....

c $(-10)^2 + 4 \times 6$ ....

d $20 - (-4)^2$ ....

e $81 + (-6)^2 - (3 \times -3)^2$ ....

10 Estimate the answer to each calculation.

a 18×3.2 ....

b $\sqrt{38} \times 41$ ....

Round 38 to the nearest square number, so it is easy to find the square root.

11 a Complete this number line.

$$\begin{array}{ccccc} 1 & 2 & 3 & 4 & 5 \end{array}$$

$\sqrt[3]{1} \quad \sqrt[3]{8} \quad \sqrt[3]{\rule{1cm}{0.4pt}} \quad \sqrt[3]{\rule{1cm}{0.4pt}} \quad \sqrt[3]{\rule{1cm}{0.4pt}}$

b Use the number line to estimate a value for these cube roots.

i $\sqrt[3]{6}$ ....

ii $\sqrt[3]{43}$ ....

iii $\sqrt[3]{70}$ ....

12 Work out

a $(-3)^3$ ....

b $-10 \times (-5)^3$ ....

c $2^3 - (-2)^3$ ....

13 Here are four number cards.

$\sqrt{11 + 5^2}$ $15 - (1 + \sqrt[3]{27})$ $5 \times 1^2(\sqrt[3]{64})$ $\sqrt{-9} \div -1$

a Work out the mean of the values of the number cards.

b Work out the range of the values of the number cards.

14 Problem-solving   The sum of these two values is 10. Work out the missing number.

$\dfrac{4^2 - \sqrt{64}}{1^3}$ $\dfrac{20 - ....}{3^2}$

15 Reasoning   Maggie and Jack work out $100 - (-5)^2$ and $100 - 5^2$. Maggie says, 'I get the same answer for both.' Jack says, 'I get different answers.' Who is correct? Complete this sentence to explain.

.... is correct because ....

16 STEM / Reasoning   The distance travelled by an object is related to its acceleration and the time taken. Jeremy works out the distance travelled by a car using the rule

$$\text{distance} = \frac{\text{acceleration} \times \text{time}^2}{2}$$

Car	A	B	C
Acceleration (m/s^2)	15	10	15
Time (seconds)	20	15	40
Distance (m)			

a Work out the distance travelled by each car.

b Car C has the same acceleration as car A. It has travelled for twice the time of car A.

Has it travelled twice as far? ....

$\text{distance} = \dfrac{15 \times 20^2}{2}$

$= \square$

21

2 Unit test

PROGRESS BAR Colour in the progress bar as you get questions correct. Then fill in the progression chart on pages 107-109.

1 a What is the highest common factor of 16 and 18? _____

b Is your answer to part **a** a prime number? _____

2 a What is the lowest common multiple of 3 and 7? _____

b Is your answer to part **a** a prime number? _____

3 Work out

a $868 \div 14$ _____ **b** $911 \div 22$ _____ **c** $5 \div 6$ _____

4 Work out

a $12 + -6$ _____ **b** $-5 - 6$ _____ **c** $8 - -7$ _____

5 Work out an estimate for $\sqrt{18}$. _____

6 Write down both answers to $\sqrt{49}$. _____

7 Work out

a 2×4^3 _____ **b** $\dfrac{2^3}{2^2}$ _____ **c** $8 \times \sqrt[3]{27} + 6$ _____

8 Work out

a 15×-2 _____ **b** -8×-8 _____

c $5 \times (-3)^2$ _____ **d** $(-5)^3 \times -2$ _____

9 Estimate the answer to each calculation.

a $29 \times 12 + 48 \times 23$ _____

b $32.7 + \dfrac{16.1}{5.2}$ _____

10 Use the fact that

a $324 = 9 \times 36$ to work out $\sqrt{324}$. _____

b $-1728 = -27 \times 64$ to work out $\sqrt[3]{-1728}$. _____

11 Work out

a $\dfrac{3^3 - 3^2}{6}$ _____ **b** $\dfrac{62 + \sqrt[3]{1000}}{6^2}$ _____

3.1 Simplifying algebraic expressions

1 Simplify

a $p + p + p$

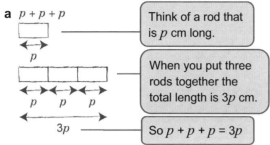

Think of a rod that is p cm long.

When you put three rods together the total length is $3p$ cm.

So $p + p + p = 3p$

An algebraic expression, for example, $3x + 2y$, contains numbers and letters. Each part of an algebraic expression is called a term.
Like terms contain the same letter (or do not contain a letter).

Worked example

b $w + w + w + w + w$ .... **c** $3p + 4p$ .... **d** $5w - 2w$ ....

2 Simplify by collecting like terms.

a $3t + 2t + 5 = 5t +$ .... **b** $5w - 3w + 2y$ ....

c $5h + 2h + 5j + 2 = 7h +$ .... + ... **d** $7h + 1 - 4h + 2$ ....

You simplify an expression by collecting like terms.

3 Simplify

a $t \times t$ ....

b $n \times n \times n$ ....

c $i \times i \times i \times i$ ....

$2 \times 2 \times 2 = 2^3$
In the same way we can write $t \times t \times t = t^3$

4 Simplify

a $3d^2 + 5d^2 = 8$ .... **b** $5b^2 + 4b^2 + 3b =$ .... $+ 3b$

c $7h^3 + 3h + 2h^3$ .... **d** $4c + 4c^2 + 4c$ ....

e $6k^5 - k^5$ .... **f** $6m^2 + 4m^3 - 3m^3$ ....

Like terms must have *exactly* the same letters and powers.
For example, $2x^2$ and $3x^3$ are *not* like terms as the powers of x are different.

5 Simplify

a $b \times c$ .... **b** $a \times a \times c \times c$ ....

c $s \times 3$ .... **d** $d \times 3 \times c$ ....

Write letters in alphabetical order.
$n \times m = mn$
Write numbers before letters.
$a \times 2 = 2 \times a = 2a$

6 Simplify

a $5c \times 3c = 5 \times c \times 3 \times c$

$= 5 \times 3 \times c \times c$

$= ....c^2$

The order of multiplication does not matter.

b $2d \times 7d$ ....

c $\frac{10b}{5} = 2b$

$\frac{10b}{5}$ means $10b \div 5$.
Work out $10 \div 5$

d $\frac{18t}{6}$ ....

7 Write ≡ between equivalent expressions.

a $x + y$ .... $y + x$ **b** $x - y$ .... $y - x$

c xy .... yx **d** $x \div y$ .... $y \div x$

Test with some numerical values for x and y.

The identity symbol (≡) shows that two expressions are always equivalent.
For example, $a + 2b \equiv 2b + a$

CHECK Tick each box as your **confidence** in this topic improves.

Need extra help? Go to page 29 and tick the boxes next to Q1, 2, 4, 5 and 7. Then have a go at them once you've finished 3.1–3.6.

3.2 Writing algebraic expressions

1 Hannah collects football cards. She has c cards.
Write an expression for how many she has when there are

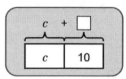

a 10 more ....

b 7 fewer ....

c 12 fewer ....

d twice as many ....

e 4 times as many ....

f half as many. ....

Finding half is the same as dividing by 2.

2 a Barney has f football cards and r rugby cards.
Write an expression for the total number of football and rugby cards he has. ....

b Barney gives away 5 football cards and is given 3 rugby cards.
Write an expression for the total number of football and rugby cards he has now. ....

Try it with numbers. How would you write 5 more than 3?

3 Write an algebraic expression for

a d more than c ....

b c multiplied by d ....

c d less than c ....

d d more than 7 times c ....

e 5 times d add 3 times c ....

f c multiplied by itself ....

g 9 times d multiplied by itself ....

h 1 less than c multiplied by itself ....

i c divided by d ....

j 7 more than 9 divided by c. ....

4 Write an expression for the output of each function machine.

a is multiplied by 3 then 5 is added.

a Input → Output

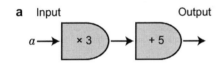

b Input → Output

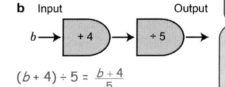

$a \times 3 + 5 = 3a + 5$

$(b + 4) \div 5 = \dfrac{b + 4}{5}$

To show that the whole expression is divided by 5 draw a long division line.

c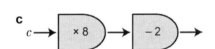

d

e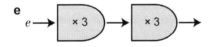

f

Guided

5 A rectangle has width w. The height is 2 more than the width.

a Write an expression for the height. ....

b Write and simplify an expression for the perimeter.

w

c Calculate the perimeter of the rectangle when $w = 8$ cm.

CHECK Tick each box as your **confidence** in this topic improves.

Need extra help? Go to page 30 and tick the boxes next to Q15 and 16. Then have a go at them once you've finished 3.1–3.6.

3.3 STEM: Using formulae

1 Work out the value of each expression when $a = 5$.

 a $3a = 3 \times a = 3 \times 5 = 15$ **b** $7a$ _____ **c** $a + 7$ _____

 d $a - 7$ _____ **e** a^2 _____ **f** $9 - a$ _____

Worked example

2 Given $a = 3$, $b = 4$ and $c = 6$ work out the value of

 a ab _____ **b** $ac + 2$ _____ **c** $3(b + 1)$ _____

 d $2(a + c)$ _____ **e** $\dfrac{c}{2}$ _____ **f** $\dfrac{b+c}{5}$ _____

3 STEM Use the formula density = $\dfrac{\text{mass}}{\text{volume}}$ to work out the density of

 a a piece of plastic with a mass of 12 g and a volume of 6 cm^3

> A **formula** is a general rule for a relationship between quantities. You use a formula to work out an unknown quantity by substituting.

 density = $\dfrac{12}{6}$

> Substitute the values into the formula. Write the units. g/cm^3 means grams per cubic cm.

   = 2 g/cm^3

> **Literacy hint**
> Density is the mass (in grams) of 1 cm^3 of a substance.

 b a lump of metal with a mass of 28 g and a volume of 8 cm^3

 c a sample of liquid with a mass of 250 g and a volume of 200 cm^3.

4 STEM Use the formula distance = speed × time to work out the distance travelled when

 a speed = 20 m/s, time = 4 seconds

> m/s means metres per second.
> km/h means kilometres per hour.
> mph means miles per hour.

 distance = 20 × 4 = _____ metres

 b speed = 5 m/s, time = 30 seconds _____

 c speed = 50 km/h, time = 2 hours _____

 d speed = 4 mph, time = $\frac{1}{2}$ hour. _____

5 STEM The formula for converting from temperature in Celsius (C) to Fahrenheit (F) is
$F = 1.8C + 32$.

Convert these temperatures into °F.

 a 100°C _____ **b** 0°C _____

 c −100°C _____ **d** −40°C _____

6 STEM The energy a body possess due to its motion is worked out using the formula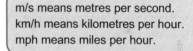

 energy = $\dfrac{\text{mass} \times \text{velocity}^2}{2}$.

> Energy is measured in joules (J).
> Mass is in kg and velocity in m/s.

Work out the energy of

 a a car with a mass of 1500 kg and a velocity of 20 m/s _____

 b an athlete with a mass of 95 kg running at 12.2 m/s. _____

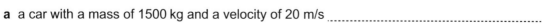

CHECK Tick each box as your **confidence** in this topic improves.

Need extra help? Go to pages 29–30 and tick the boxes next to Q10, 11, 12 and 13. Then have a go at them once you've finished 3.1–3.6.

3.4 Writing formulae

1 A mobile phone company charges £0.25 per minute for talk time and £2.50 per gigabyte (GB) for downloads. It uses the formula $C = 0.25t + 2.5d$.

  a What do you think t stands for? ....

  b What do you think d stands for? ....

  c How much would 100 minutes of talk time and 2 GB of downloads cost? ....

2 Renting a car costs £15 per day.

  a How much does it cost to rent a car for 4 days?

  £15 × 4 = £60

  b How much does it cost to rent a car for a week?

> Write down the cost per day.
> Multiply the cost by the number of days.

> **Literacy hint**
> 'per day' means each day.

  c Write an expression for how much a car costs to rent for d days. $15d$

  d Write a formula for the cost, C, of renting a car for d days. $C =$ ....

3 Davina organises birthday parties. She always orders 5 more party bags than the number of guests. Write a formula that connects the number of guests, g, to the number of party bags, b.

4 Modelling

  a Write an algebraic expression for finding the mean of 4 numbers a, b, c and d. ....

  b Write a formula for the mean of 4 numbers.

> mean of 4 numbers = $\dfrac{\text{sum of 4 numbers}}{4}$

  c Use your formula to work out the mean when $a = 2$, $b = 5$, $c = 6$ and $d = 7$.

> Write $m = \square$

5 Real / STEM The mean total lung volume is worked out from 3 different readings.
The readings are p, q and r.
Write a formula to work out the mean total lung volume, T.

6 A function machine multiplies each input by 2 and then adds 7.

  a What is the output if the input is

  i 5 ....   **ii** –4 ....   **iii** a? ....

> Draw the function machine.

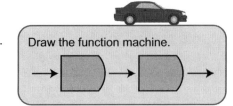

  b Write a formula which connects the

   output, b, with the input, a. ....

7 A taxi charges £1.25 a mile plus an extra £4.

  a How much does a 3 mile taxi ride cost? ....

  b Write a formula which connects the charge, C, to the distance travelled, d.

CHECK Tick each box as your **confidence** in this topic improves.

Need extra help? Go to page 30 and tick the boxes next to Q17 and 18. Then have a go at them once you've finished 3.1–3.6.

1 Expand

  a $3(y + 5) = 3 \times y + 3 \times 5 = 3y +$ ....

  b $7(h - 2) = 7 \times h - 7 \times 2 =$ ....

  c $2(d + 10)$ ....

  d $5(p - 5)$ ....

  e $2(2 + k)$ ....

> **Expand** a bracket means multiply every number inside the bracket by the number or letter outside the bracket.

2 A company making hockey sticks works out their profit, P, by subtracting £17 from the cost of a hockey stick, H, and multiplying the answer by the number of hockey sticks sold, a.

  Write a formula for calculating P. ....

3 Expand

  a $t(t + 2) = t \times t + t \times 2 = t^2 +$ ....   **b** $d(d + 5)$ ....

  c $s(s - 3)$ ....   **d** $y(5y + 3) = y \times 5y + y \times 3 = 5y^2$ ....

  e $j(5 - 7j)$ ....   **f** $3q(2q + 4) = 3q \times 2q + 3q \times 4 = 6q^2$ ....

  g $5t(5t - 1)$ ....   **h** $3x(10 - 3x)$ ....

4 Work out the value of the expressions when $p = 2$ and $q = 6$.

> Remember to follow the priority of operations.

Worked example

  a p^2 ....   **b** $p^2 + 6$ ....

  c $5p^2$ ....   **d** $p^2 + q^2$ ....

  e $(5p)^2$ ....   **f** $(p + q)^2$ ....

  g $2q^2 + 4p$ ....   **h** $2q^2 - 10p^2$ ....

  i $\dfrac{5q}{2}$ ....   **j** $\dfrac{q^2}{2}$ ....

  k $\left(\dfrac{q}{6}\right)^2$ ....

5 Sharon has £x. Kate has the square of Sharon's amount. Meinir has £10 more than Kate.

  a Write an expression for Kate's money. ....

  b Write an expression for Meinir's money. ....

  c Write and simplify an expression for the sum of all their money. ....

  d Sharon has £5. What is the sum of their money? ....

6 Work out the value of the expressions when $g = 2$ and $h = 5$.

  a $g^3 + 10$ .... $\boxed{g^3 + 10 = g \times g \times g + 10}$ **b** $h^3 - 20$ ....

  c $g^3 + h^3$ ....   **d** $4g^3$ ....   **e** $(2h)^3$ ....

  f $(h - 1)^3$ ....   **g** $(g + 1)^2$ ....   **h** $(2h - 9)^5$ ....

  i $\dfrac{g^3}{4}$ ....   **j** $\dfrac{g^4}{2}$ ....   **k** $2g^3 + h$ ....

CHECK   Tick each box as your **confidence** in this topic improves.

Need extra help? Go to pages 29–30 and tick the boxes next to Q3, 6 and 14. Then have a go at them once you've finished 3.1–3.6.

Guided

1 Write down the common factors of

a 6 and $4p$

Factors of 6: 1, 2, 3, 6

Factors of $4p$: 1, 2, 4, p, $2p$, $4p$

Common factors of 6 and $4p$: 1, 2

b $6x$ and 10

c 9 and $12t$

> Expanding removes brackets from an expression. **Factorising** inserts brackets into an expression.
>
> expand
>
>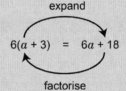
>
> $6(a + 3)$ = $6a + 18$
>
> factorise
>
> To factorise $6a + 18$, write the common factor of its terms, 6, outside the brackets. This is called 'taking out the common factor'.

2 Write down the HCF of

a $6t$ and 12 ....

b 14 and $21x$ ....

Guided

3 Complete these factorisations.

a $5x + 15 = 5(..... + 3)$ —

> 5 is a common factor of both $5x$ and 15.
> Write 5 in front of the bracket.
> Divide both terms by 5 to work out the values in the bracket.

b $14x + 7 = 7(..... + ...)$

c $6x - 9 = 3(..... - .....)$ **d** $10x - 15 = 5(..... - .....)$ **e** $18x + 6 = ... (3x + ...)$

f $25x - 5 = ... (5x - .....)$ **g** $4x + 12$ ....   **h** $27 - 9x$ ....

4 Factorise each expression.

> Check your factorisation by expanding the brackets.

Worked example

a $5x + 20$ ....   **b** $3x - 12$ ....

c $20x - 10$ ....   **d** $5x - 25$ ....

e $12 + 6x$ ....   **f** $9 - 36x$ ....

5 How many different ways can the expression $6x + 12$ be factorised?

> To factorise completely, write the highest common factor outside the brackets.

6 Factorise completely.

a $4x + 6$ ....   **b** $9t + 12$ ....

c $16g + 32$ ....   **d** $20d - 5$ ....

e $8 - 4w$ ....   **f** $8 + 18x$ ....

g $120q + 40$ ....   **h** $44 + 22y$ ....

7 Factorise completely.

a $6a + 2b + 8$ ....

b $20 + 30p + 15q$ ....

c $ab + 3a + 9a$ ....

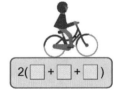

$2(\Box + \Box + \Box)$

CHECK   Tick each box as your **confidence** in this topic improves.

Need extra help? Go to page 29 and tick the boxes next to Q8 and 9. Then have a go at them once you've finished 3.1–3.6.

28

3 Strengthen

Simplifying expressions

1 Complete

   a $t + t + t =$ .... t **b** $p + p + p + p =$ .... p

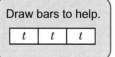
Draw bars to help.

| t | t | t |

2 Simplify

   a $2n + 3n = 5$ ....   **b** $6a + 3a$ ....

   c $9q - q = 9q - 1q =$ ....   **d** $3b + b$ ....

   e $3g + 2 + 4g = 3g + 4g + 2 = 7g +$ ....   **f** $6s + 5t - 2s$ ....

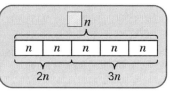

3 Expand

   a $3(n + 4) = (n + 4) + (n + 4) + (n + 4) = 3n +$ ....

   b $2(p + 5) = (p + 5) + (p + 5) =$ ....

   c $4(a + 3)$ ....

   d $5(4 - b)$ ....

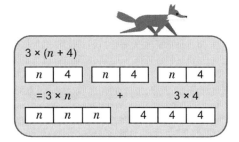

4 Fill in the missing numbers.

   a $5 \times 5 \times 5 = 5^{.....}$ **b** $t \times t \times t \times t \times t = t^{.....}$

5 Simplify $6p \times 3p$ ....

6 Expand

   a $n(n + 2) = n \times n + n \times 2 = n^2 +$ ....   **b** $t(t + 3)$ ....

   c $p(5 + p)$ ....   **d** $g(1 - g)$ ....

$n \times n$
$n(n + 2)$
$n \times 2$

7 Simplify by collecting like terms.

   a $a^2 + a^2 + 5a =$ ..... $a^2 +$ ....   **b** $5b + b^2 + 4b$ ....

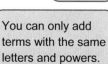
You can only add terms with the same letters and powers.

8 a What is the highest common factor (HCF) of 2 and 6? ....

   b Complete the factorisation. $2a + 6 =$ ..... (.....+.....)

Find the HCF first.

9 Complete the factorisation. $3a + 15 =$ ..... (..... + ...)

The HCF is outside the bracket.

Substitution

10 The formula to work out the distance a train travels is distance = speed × time.
A train travels at a speed of 100 km per hour for 3 hours.

How far does it travel?

distance = speed × time

      = $100 \times 3 =$ ...... km

11 Work out the value of each expression when $x = 4$ and $y = 8$.

a $x + 6$ .... | $x + 6$ | **b** $y - 5$ .... | **c** $x + y$ ....
| $4 + 6 = \square$ |

d $10x$ .... **e** $xy + 3$ .... **f** $\frac{y}{2}$ ....

12 $T = 4(p + q)$. Work out the value of T when $p = 5$ and $q = 3$.

13 Use the formula $T = 4 + p$ to work out the value of T when

a $p = -2$ .... **b** $p = -4$ ....

> $T = 4 + -2$
> $= 4 - 2$

14 Complete the calculations when $n = 2$.

a $n^3 = 2 \times$ ...... $\times$ ...... $=$ ...... **b** $n^2 + 5 =$ ...... $\times$ ...... $+ 5 =$ ......

c $n^4 =$ ...... $\times$ ...... $\times$ ...... $\times$ ...... $=$ ...... **d** $5n^2$ ....

> Remember to calculate powers first.

Writing expressions and formulae

15 Match each algebraic expression to its description.

| $x + 5$ | | $x - 5$ | | $5 - x$ | | $5x$ | | $\frac{x}{5}$ |

| 5 times x | | 5 less than x | | 5 more than x | | One fifth of x | | x less than 5 |

16 Write a description for each expression.

a $a + b$ ....

b ab ....

c $b - a$ ....

d $\frac{a}{b}$ ....

> Use these phrases:
> *more than, less than, multiplied by, divided by.*
> For example, b more than ....

17 To convert from cm, C, to inches, I, multiply by 4 then divide by 10.

Write the formula. ....

18 I think of a number, add 12, and then divide by 9.

a What would the result be if the original number was 15? ....

b Complete the function machine.

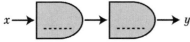

c Which of these formulae correctly connects x with y?

$y = 12x + 9$ $\qquad$ $y = \frac{x + 12}{9}$ $\qquad$ $y = 9(x + 12)$ $\qquad$ $y = \frac{x}{12} + 9$

1 A hexagon has sides of length x.
Write and simplify an expression for its perimeter.

2 The surface area of a cube, A, can be found using the formula $A = 6e^2$ where e = edge length.

   a Work out the surface area of a cube with an edge length of 5 cm. ....

   b The surface area of a cube is 54 cm^2. Work out its edge length. ....

3 Finance A party organising company uses the formula $P = 4.5c + 6a$
for calculating profit, where c is the number of children and a is the number of adults.

Work out the profit when there are

   a 20 children and 10 adults ....

   b 30 adults. ....

4 A quadrilateral has one side of length y cm.
The second side is 2 cm more than double this length.
The other two sides are each 3 times the length of the second side.
Write an expression for the perimeter of the quadrilateral.
Simplify your expression as much as possible.

Sketch and label
the quadrilateral.

5 In the pyramid each brick is the sum of the two bricks below.
Work out the missing expressions.

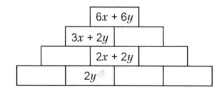

6 A maths teacher uses this number puzzle: *Think of a number. Double it. Add 2. Multiply by 5.*
Subtract 10 times the number you first thought of. Your answer is 10.
Explain the teacher's trick.

Call the unknown number 'x' and
construct an algebraic expression.

7 When $x = -3$, all but one of these expressions have the same value.
Which is the 'odd one out'?

| $x^2 + 4$ | | $2x + 19$ | | $-\dfrac{39}{x}$ | | $2x - 7$ | | $-4x + 1$ |

8 The product of two terms is $12x^2$.

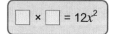

$\square \times \square = 12x^2$

   a What could the two terms be? ....

   b Give two other possible terms. ....

9 The sum of two terms is $10x$. Their product is $24x^2$.
What are the terms?

Literacy hint
Product means multiply.

10 The length of a rectangle is 5 times the width. Write and simplify an expression for

  a the area .... **b** the perimeter. ....

Guided

11 Show the mapping $x \rightarrow x + 3$ on a pair of number lines from 0 to 10.

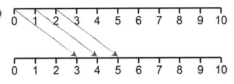

When $x = 0$, $x + 3 = 0 + 3 = 3$

When $x = 1$, $x + 3 = 1 + 3 = 4$

When $x = 2$, $x + 3 = 2 + 3 = 5$

> Substitute each number on the top number line into the function $x + 3$.

12 Show the mapping $x \rightarrow 2x - 2$ on a pair of number lines from –5 to 5.

Guided

13 a Complete the mapping diagram for $x \rightarrow \frac{1}{2}x$

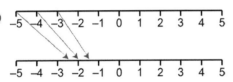

  b What value maps to 5? ......

14 The first of five consecutive whole numbers is x.

  a Write expressions for the next three numbers.

  x, $x + 1$, $x +$ ......, $x +$ ...., $x +$ ......

  b Write and simplify an expression for the sum of the five numbers.

> **Literacy hint**
> Consecutive numbers follow each other.
> 4, 5, 6 are consecutive.

  c Factorise the expression. ....

  d Write an expression for the mean of the five numbers. ....

   What do you notice?

15 The first of three consecutive whole even numbers is x.
Write an expression for the mean of the three numbers.

> Look at Q14.

16 What value(s) of x would make each of these statements true?

  a $3x < x$ .... **b** $x^2 = 3x$ ....

  c $x^2 > 3x$ .... **d** $x^2 < 3x$ ....

3 Unit test

PROGRESS BAR Colour in the progress bar as you get questions correct.
Then fill in the progression chart on pages 107-109.

1 To convert between days and hours use the formula

Hours = number of days × 24

Work out the number of hours in 5 days. ....

2 The formula for calculating the perimeter of a shape, P, is $P = 2x + 5y$.
Work out the value of P when $x = 12$ and $y = 3$.

3 Use the formula $T = \dfrac{h(h-1)}{3}$ to work out the value of T when $h = 6$.

4 Expand $5(p - 3)$. ....

5 Write an expression for

a 5 less than t ....   **b** 4 times w ....   **c** p divided by 3. ....

6 Sophia jogs or swims every day. When she jogs she covers 1 mile. When she swims she covers 3 miles. Write a formula connecting the total distance she travels, T, with the number of days she jogs, j, and the number of days she swims, s.

7 Work out the value of these expressions when $x = 2$ and $y = 5$.

a $3(x + 4)$ ....   **b** $2(5x + y)$ ....

8 By collecting like terms, simplify $4 + 3e - 1 + 2e$. ....

9 Simplify

a $t \times t \times t \times t$ ....   **b** $2p \times p$ ....   **c** $2y \times 3y$ ....

10 By collecting like terms, simplify $2v^3 + 3v^2 + 4v^3$. ....

11 Expand $5d(3d + 3)$. ....

12 What is the value of x^2 when $x = 8$?

13 Find the value of each expression when $p = 3$ and $q = 7$.

a p^3 ....   **b** $q^2 - p$ ....

c $(q - p)^2$ ....   **d** $\dfrac{3p+q}{4}$ ....

14 Factorise

a $3d - 12$ ....   **b** $12e + 16$ ....   **c** $15 - 10f$ ....

4.1 Working with fractions

1 Sort these fractions into pairs of equivalent fractions.

$$\frac{1}{4} \quad \frac{4}{8} \quad \frac{2}{3} \quad \frac{3}{12} \quad \frac{6}{10} \quad \frac{1}{2} \quad \frac{6}{9} \quad \frac{3}{5}$$

> Equivalent fractions have the same value.

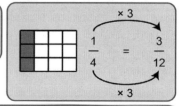

2 Problem-solving

Which is larger, $\frac{2}{3}$ or $\frac{4}{5}$? ....

> For Q2, shade in parts of the grids. Use equivalent fractions to help you.
>
> $$\frac{2}{3} = \frac{...}{15} \qquad \frac{4}{5} = \frac{...}{15}$$

3 Simplify

a

$$\frac{15}{20} \xrightarrow{\div 5} = \frac{3}{...} \xleftarrow{\div 5}$$

> You can write a fraction in its simplest form by dividing the numerator and denominator by their highest common factor (HCF) to give an equivalent fraction.

b $\frac{3}{15}$ ....

c $\frac{27}{63}$ ....

4 A shop sells 60 pasties. 45 of them are vegetarian.
What fraction are vegetarian pasties?
Write your answer in its simplest form.

5 Work out

 Guided

a $\frac{1}{2}$ of £10 = £10 ÷ 2 = ...

b $\frac{1}{10}$ of 50 kg ....

c $\frac{1}{4}$ of 80 m*l* ....

d $\frac{3}{4}$ of 80 m*l* ....

e $\frac{4}{5}$ of £30 ....

> You worked out $\frac{1}{4}$ of 80 m*l* in part **c**, now multiply by 3 for part **d**.

6 Problem-solving A bottle contains 500 m*l* of water. Rees drinks half of the water.
Owen drinks $\frac{2}{5}$ of what is left. How much does Owen drink?

> Work out half of 500 first.

7 STEM The pie chart shows the composition of a fertiliser.
What fraction of the fertiliser is

a phosphorus

b nitrogen

c other?

> How many degrees are there altogether in a pie chart? Simplify your answer.

Fertiliser composition

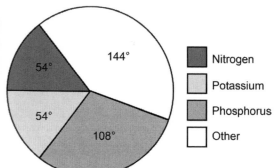

144°
54°
54°
108°

Nitrogen
Potassium
Phosphorus
Other

CHECK Tick each box as your **confidence** in this topic improves.

Need extra help? Go to page 39 and tick the boxes next to Q1, 2 and 3. Then have a go at them once you've finished 4.1– 4.5.

4.2 Adding and subtracting fractions

1 Which is larger, $1\frac{3}{4}$ or $\frac{9}{4}$?

$9 \div 4 = 2$ remainder 1, so $\frac{9}{4} = 2\frac{...}{4}$

.... is larger than ....

> A mixed number has a whole number part and a fraction part. In an improper fraction the numerator is greater than the denominator.
> A fraction greater than 1 can be written as a mixed number or an improper fraction.

2 Write these improper fractions as mixed numbers.

a $\frac{9}{5}$ ....

b $\frac{13}{4}$ ....

c $\frac{27}{2}$ ....

Worked example

3 Work out these. Give each answer in its simplest form.

a $\frac{1}{4} + \frac{1}{4} = \frac{2}{4} = \frac{1}{2}$ (÷2)

b $\frac{5}{12} + \frac{3}{12}$

c $\frac{9}{16} - \frac{5}{16}$

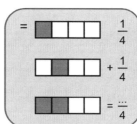

> When two fractions have the same denominator, add or subtract by adding or subtracting the numerators.

4 Work out these. Give each answer in its simplest form.

a $\frac{1}{12} + \frac{3}{4} = \frac{1}{12} + \frac{...}{12} = \frac{...}{12} = \frac{...}{...}$

b $\frac{9}{10} - \frac{2}{5}$

c $\frac{9}{14} - \frac{1}{2}$

$= \frac{3}{4} = \frac{...}{12}$ so $\frac{1}{12} + \frac{...}{12}$

> When two fractions have different denominators, first write them as equivalent fractions with the same denominator (**common denominator**).

5 Work out these. Give each answer in its simplest form.

a $\frac{1}{2} + \frac{1}{5}$

b $\frac{7}{8} - \frac{1}{6}$

Work out the LCM of 2 and 5.

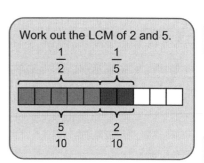

$\frac{1}{2}$ $\frac{1}{5}$

$\frac{5}{10}$ $\frac{2}{10}$

6 Work out these. Give your answers as mixed numbers.

a $\frac{1}{2} + \frac{5}{7}$

b $\frac{7}{2} + \frac{3}{4}$

c $\frac{4}{5} + \frac{5}{6}$

d $\frac{1}{2} + \frac{2}{3} + \frac{3}{5}$

$\frac{1}{2} + \frac{2}{3} + \frac{3}{5} = \frac{...}{30} + \frac{...}{30} + \frac{...}{30}$

CHECK   Tick each box as your **confidence** in this topic improves.

Need extra help? Go to page 39 and tick the box next to Q4. Then have a go at it once you've finished 4.1– 4.5.

4.3 Fractions, decimals and percentages

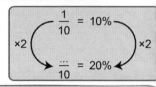

1 Complete this table of equivalent fractions, decimals and percentages.

Fraction	$\frac{1}{10}$			$\frac{2}{5}$			$\frac{7}{10}$	
Decimal		0.2		0.3	0.5			0.75
Percentage			25%			60%		

> **Equivalent** fractions, decimals and percentages have the same value. You can convert a fraction to a decimal by dividing the numerator by the denominator.

2 Complete this table.

Mixed number	$1\frac{1}{4}$					$1\frac{4}{5}$	
Decimal		1.4			1.7		
Percentage			175%	150%			

> When a positive mixed number is greater than 1, its decimal equivalent is greater than 1, and its percentage equivalent is greater than 100%.
> For example, $1\frac{2}{5} = 1.4 = 140\%$

3 Write these fractions as decimals.

a $\frac{5}{8}$

$$\frac{0.6\ldots}{8\overline{)5.0^20\,0}}$$

b $\frac{3}{20}$ ....

c $\frac{15}{4}$ ....

d $\frac{45}{75} = \frac{\ldots}{\ldots}$

Worked example

4 Last season, the Year 7 hockey team drew 7 out of their 20 matches.

a What fraction of their games did they draw? ....

b Write your answer to part **a** as a decimal. ....

c What percentage of their games did they draw? ....

5 **Modelling / STEM** Some groups of chicken eggs were hatched in incubators at different temperatures. The table shows the incubator temperature, the number of eggs in each group and the number of eggs that hatched successfully.

Incubator	A	B	C	D	E
Temperature (°C)	36.5	37.0	37.5	38.0	38.5
Number incubated	200	150	275	320	280
Number hatched	164	126	260	288	230

> **Literacy hint**
> An egg incubator is a type of heated box to keep eggs at the right temperature for hatching.

a What fraction of each group hatched successfully?

b Gerry says, 'The best temperature to hatch chicken eggs is 38.0°C'. Is Gerry correct? Explain.

6 Use the fact that $\frac{1}{50} = 0.02$ to write these fractions as decimals.

a $\frac{1}{500}$ ....

b $\frac{1}{25}$ ....

c $\frac{1}{250}$ ....

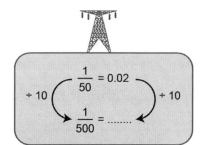

CHECK Tick each box as your **confidence** in this topic improves.

Need extra help? Go to page 39 and tick the boxes next to Q5, 6 and 7. Then have a go at them once you've finished 4.1– 4.5.

1 Work out these fractions of amounts. Write each answer as a mixed number in its simplest form.

a $\frac{3}{5}$ of 8 kg

> 8 ÷ 5 isn't a whole number, so work out 3 × 8 first.

$\frac{3}{5} \times 8 = \frac{3 \times 8}{5}$

$= \frac{24}{5} = \text{.........} $ kg

> Divide 24 by 5 and write your answer as a mixed number in its simplest form.

b $\frac{5}{9}$ of 40 m

2 Work out

a $1 \div \frac{1}{6} = 1 \times \frac{6}{1} = 6$

b $5 \div \frac{1}{2} = 5 \times \frac{2}{1} = 5 \times \text{......} = \text{......}$

c $5 \div \frac{3}{4} = 5 \times \frac{4}{3} = \frac{5 \times \text{......}}{\text{......}} = \text{.........}$

d $20 \div \frac{5}{8}$ ....

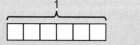
> How many sixths are there in 1?

> To divide by a fraction, you can turn the fraction upside down and multiply instead.

3 Work out these multiplications. Write each answer in its simplest form.

a $\frac{1}{2} \times \frac{1}{5} = \frac{1 \times 1}{2 \times 5} = \text{.................}$

b $\frac{1}{3} \times \frac{6}{7} = \frac{1 \times 6}{3 \times 7} = \text{......} = \text{.........}$

c $\frac{4}{9} \times \frac{1}{2}$ ....

d $\frac{3}{5} \times \frac{3}{5}$ ....

> To multiply two fractions, multiply their numerators and multiply their denominators.

> You can cancel common factors before multiplying fractions.

4 $\frac{3}{4}$ of the dogs in a dog training class are Labradors.

$\frac{2}{5}$ of the Labradors are female.

What fraction of the dogs in the class are female Labradors?

5 Fran uses this method to multiply $\frac{5}{6} \times \frac{8}{15}$.

$\frac{5}{6} \times \frac{8}{15} = \frac{5 \times 8}{6 \times 15} = \frac{{}^{1}\cancel{5} \times {}^{4}\cancel{8}}{{}_{3}\cancel{6} \times \cancel{15}_{3}} = \frac{4}{9}$

> **Worked example**
>

Use Fran's method to work out these multiplications.

a $\frac{2}{5} \times \frac{15}{16}$ ....

b $\frac{3}{8} \times \frac{2}{21}$ ....

6 Work out these divisions.
Write each answer in its simplest form.

a $\frac{1}{4} \div \frac{7}{12} = \frac{1}{4} \times \frac{12}{7} = \frac{\text{.....}}{\text{.....}}$

b $\frac{4}{21} \div \frac{4}{7} = \frac{4}{21} \times \frac{\text{.....}}{\text{.....}} = \frac{\text{.....}}{\text{.....}}$

c $\frac{3}{5} \div \frac{18}{25}$ ....

d $\frac{2}{5} \div \frac{8}{9}$ ....

> Turn the fraction you are dividing by upside down and multiply.

CHECK Tick each box as your **confidence** in this topic improves.

Need extra help? Go to page 40 and tick the boxes next to Q8 –12. Then have a go at them once you've finished 4.1– 4.5.

1 a Write each time as a mixed number.

  i 1 hour 45 minutes _____

  ii 5 hours 10 minutes _____

b Use your calculator to add your answers in part **a**. _____

> 1 minute is $\frac{1}{60}$ of an hour.

2 Write these improper fractions as decimals.

 Guided

a $\frac{21}{5} = 4 \frac{\ldots}{\ldots} = 4$ _____

b $\frac{11}{4} = \ldots \frac{\ldots}{\ldots} =$ _____

> Write as a mixed number first. Then write the fraction part as a decimal.

3 Work out these additions. Write your answer in its simplest form.

Guided

a $1\frac{3}{8} + 2\frac{1}{2} = 1 + 2 + \frac{3}{8} + \frac{1}{2} = 3 + \frac{3}{8} + \frac{\ldots}{8} =$ _____

b $7\frac{2}{3} + 5\frac{2}{9}$ _____

c $8\frac{7}{8} + 5\frac{5}{12}$ _____

> When you add mixed numbers, add the whole numbers first, then add the fraction parts.

4 Work out these subtractions. Write each answer in its simplest form.

 Guided

a $6\frac{1}{2} - 2\frac{2}{5} = \frac{13}{2} - \frac{12}{5}$

> Write the mixed numbers as improper fractions.

$= \frac{\ldots}{10} - \frac{\ldots}{10} = \frac{\ldots}{10} =$ ....

> Write fractions with a common denominator, and then subtract.
> Then write your answer as a mixed number.

b $11\frac{1}{6} - 8\frac{5}{6}$

c $7\frac{2}{9} - 5\frac{1}{6}$

5 Harold works out the range of $1\frac{9}{10}$, $3\frac{7}{8}$, $1\frac{5}{12}$, $2\frac{3}{11}$, $3\frac{1}{3}$ as $3\frac{1}{3} - 1\frac{9}{10} = 1\frac{13}{20}$.
He is wrong.
Work out the correct range.

6 Work out these.
Write each answer in its simplest form.

 Guided

a $4\frac{1}{2} \times 3 = \frac{9}{2} \times 3 = \frac{9 \times 3}{2} = \frac{\ldots}{2} = \ldots \frac{\ldots}{2}$

b $7 \times 2\frac{2}{3}$ _____

7 Work out these.
Write each answer in its simplest form.

a $8\frac{1}{3} \div 5$ _____

b $2\frac{3}{4} \div \frac{2}{3}$ _____

> **Worked example**
>
>

CHECK Tick each box as your **confidence** in this topic improves.

Need extra help? Go to page 40 and tick the boxes next to Q13–16. Then have a go at them once you've finished 4.1– 4.5.

38

4 Strengthen

Equivalence

☐ **1** Write each fraction in its simplest form.

a $\frac{4}{8} = \frac{2}{4} = \frac{...}{...}$ (÷2, ÷2 top; ÷2, ÷2 bottom)

> Start by dividing both numbers by 2, then check to see if you can divide again.

b $\frac{9}{12} = \frac{...}{...}$ (÷3 top; ÷3 bottom)

c $\frac{6}{18} = \frac{3}{9} = \frac{...}{...}$ (÷2, ÷... top; ÷2, ÷... bottom)

☐ **2** Out of 28 people, 8 have blue eyes.
What fraction of the people have blue eyes?

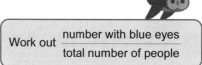

> Work out $\dfrac{\text{number with blue eyes}}{\text{total number of people}}$

☐ **3** The table shows the types of dogs in a park.

Type of dog	Mongrel	Labrador	Collie	Other
Number of dogs	36	4	2	6

a Work out the total number of dogs. ....

b What fraction of the dogs are mongrels? ....

☐ **4** Work out these. Give each answer in its simplest form.

a $\frac{1}{8} + \frac{3}{4}$ ....

b $\frac{5}{6} - \frac{4}{5}$ ....

☐ **5** Complete these equivalent fractions, decimals and percentages.

a $\frac{1}{10} = 0.1 = 10\%$
$\frac{2}{10} = ... = ...\%$ (×2)

b $\frac{1}{10} = 0.1 = 10\%$
$\frac{7}{10} = ... = ...\%$ (×.....)

c $\frac{1}{5} = 0.2 = 20\%$
$\frac{3}{5} = ... = ...\%$

☐ **6** Use your answers to Q5 to complete this table.

Fraction	$1\frac{1}{10}$	$1\frac{7}{10}$		
Decimal			2.2	
Percentage				320%

☐ **7** Write these fractions as decimals.

a $\frac{3}{8} = 3 \div 8$

b $\frac{5}{8}$

$\begin{array}{r} 0.\,3\,...\,... \\ 8\overline{)3.^30^60\ 0} \end{array}$

Worked example

Multiplying and dividing with fractions

☐ **8** Work out

    a $\frac{3}{4}$ of £20 ....   **b** $\frac{5}{6}$ of 18 kg ....

☐ **9** Work out

> $\frac{2}{5}$ × 35 = $\frac{2}{5}$ of 35
> Work out $\frac{1}{5}$ of 35,
> then multiply by 2.

    a $\frac{2}{5}$ × 35   **b** 21 × $\frac{2}{3}$

☐ **10** Work out

> $\frac{1}{4}$ of 17 isn't a whole number.
> Multiply then simplify.

    a $\frac{3}{4}$ of 17 m = $\frac{3 \times 17}{4}$ = $\frac{51}{4}$, 51 ÷ 4 = 12 r ..... = 12$\frac{...}{4}$ m

    b $\frac{2}{5}$ of 23 g = $\frac{2 \times 23}{....}$ = ...

☐ **11** Work out

    a $\frac{3}{4}$ × $\frac{2}{7}$ = $\frac{3 \times 2}{4 \times 7}$ = $\frac{.....}{.....}$ $\overset{÷.....}{=}$ $\frac{.....}{.....}$

> Simplify your answers
> if possible.

    b $\frac{5}{8}$ × $\frac{2}{5}$

☐ **12** Work out

> $\frac{1}{5}$ ÷ $\frac{2}{3}$ is the same as $\frac{1}{5}$ × $\frac{3}{2}$.
> Then use same method as Q11.

    a $\frac{1}{5}$ ÷ $\frac{2}{3}$ **b** $\frac{1}{4}$ ÷ $\frac{3}{7}$ **c** $\frac{3}{8}$ ÷ $\frac{9}{16}$

Working with mixed numbers

☐ **13** Write these mixed numbers as improper fractions.

    a $1\frac{2}{3}$ ....

    b $3\frac{1}{5}$ ....

Worked example

How many thirds are there?

    1         $\frac{2}{3}$

| $\frac{1}{3}$ | $\frac{1}{3}$ | $\frac{1}{3}$ | $\frac{1}{3}$ | $\frac{1}{3}$ | |

☐ **14** Write these improper fractions as mixed numbers.

    a $\frac{7}{3}$ = 7 ÷ 3 = 2 r 1, $\frac{7}{3}$ = 2$\frac{1}{...}$

> Convert to improper fractions first.
> Simplify your answer.

    b $\frac{24}{7}$ ....

☐ **15** Work out

    a $2\frac{1}{2}$ + $3\frac{3}{4}$ = $\frac{...}{2}$ + $\frac{...}{4}$ = $\frac{...}{4}$ + $\frac{...}{4}$ = $\frac{...}{4}$ = ... $\frac{...}{4}$

> Use the grid method.
>
> | × | 2 | $\frac{3}{4}$ |
> | 6 | | |

    b $2\frac{1}{3}$ + $2\frac{2}{9}$

    c $4\frac{1}{3}$ − $1\frac{5}{6}$

☐ **16** Work out

    a 6 × $2\frac{3}{4}$ **b** 10 × $1\frac{2}{3}$

4 Extend

1 Problem-solving / Reasoning Here are some fractions.

$$\frac{12}{14} \qquad \frac{10}{35} \qquad \frac{20}{28} \qquad \frac{10}{70} \qquad \frac{21}{56} \qquad \frac{9}{21} \qquad \frac{28}{49}$$

> **Strategy hint**
> Start by writing each fraction in its simplest form.

Which fraction is the odd one out? Explain your answer.

2 Complete these fraction pyramids. Each brick is the sum of the two bricks below it.

a

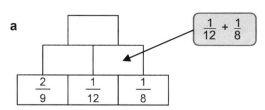

$$\frac{1}{12} + \frac{1}{8}$$

b

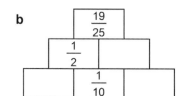

3 STEM / Problem-solving The pie chart shows the composition of goose eggs.
Work out the amounts of protein and moisture in a goose egg of mass 120 g.

> Work out the fractions of the egg that are protein and moisture first.

Composition of goose eggs

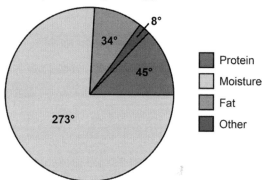

8°
34°
45°
273°

- ■ Protein
- □ Moisture
- ■ Fat
- ■ Other

4 Reasoning Omar writes the fraction $\frac{11}{18}$ as a decimal.

This is what he writes.

$$11\overline{)18.{}^{7}0{}^{4}0{}^{7}0{}^{4}0} \quad \text{so} \quad \frac{11}{18} = 1.6363...$$

with quotient 1.6363

a Explain the mistake that Omar has made. ....

b Work out the correct decimal equivalent of $\frac{11}{18}$. ....

5 Work out

a $2\frac{1}{2} + 2\frac{1}{3} + 2\frac{1}{4}$

> Simplify your answers.

b $4\frac{1}{4} + 3\frac{1}{5} - 5\frac{7}{8}$

6 STEM In a 750 ml bottle of sunflower oil there is 82 ml of saturated fat, 150 ml of monounsaturated fat and 518 ml of polyunsaturated fat.
What fraction of the sunflower oil is monounsaturated fat?
Give your fraction in its simplest form.

7 Problem-solving Sort these cards into four groups of correct calculations.
There must be one triangular, one rectangular and one circular card in each group.

Strategy hint
Start by rewriting each circle card as

$\times \dfrac{\square}{\square}$ instead of $\div \dfrac{\square}{\square}$

8 Work out these divisions.
Write each answer as a mixed number in its simplest form.

a $5 \div \dfrac{2}{5}$

b $3 \div \dfrac{9}{13}$

9 You can work out the distance, in miles, a plane travels using the formula

distance = average speed × time

Work out the distance a plane travels when

a average speed = 600 miles per hour and time = 2 hours 30 minutes

Enter the time as a mixed number on your calculator.

b average speed = 420 miles per hour and time = 4 hours 36 minutes

10 Problem-solving Complete this calculation in two different ways.

a $\boxed{}\dfrac{\square}{\square} - \dfrac{\square}{\square} = 3\dfrac{1}{6}$

b $\boxed{}\dfrac{\square}{\square} - \dfrac{\square}{\square} = 3\dfrac{1}{6}$

11 Real / Problem-solving Karl's fish tank has a leak. It leaks $\dfrac{1}{3}$ of the water in an hour.

$\dfrac{3}{4}$ of what was left leaks out in the next hour. What fraction of the water is left in the fish tank?

12 Which of these three fractions, $\dfrac{3}{16}, \dfrac{3}{8}$ or $\dfrac{3}{4}$, is the missing fraction in this calculation?

$\dfrac{3}{8} \div \dfrac{\square}{\square} = \dfrac{1}{2}$

13 These are the ages, in years, of Bert's five dogs.

$1\dfrac{1}{6}$ $1\dfrac{11}{12}$ $2\dfrac{3}{4}$ $4\dfrac{1}{3}$ $9\dfrac{1}{2}$

Work out the mean age.

4 Unit test

1 Write each fraction in its simplest form.

  a $\frac{10}{15}$ ....   **b** $\frac{9}{36}$ ....   **c** $\frac{24}{30}$ ....

2 Write these amounts in order of size, starting with the smallest.

  $\frac{5}{6}$ of £30 $\frac{1}{3}$ of £69 $\frac{2}{5}$ of £60 ....

3 Work out these. Give each answer in its simplest form.

  a $\frac{1}{2} + \frac{1}{6}$ ....   **b** $\frac{11}{15} - \frac{1}{3}$ ....

4 Write $\frac{32}{5}$ as a mixed number. ....

5 Write $5\frac{3}{7}$ as an improper fraction. ....

6 Work out $18 \times \frac{5}{6}$

7 Complete this table.

Fraction		$\frac{3}{4}$		$1\frac{3}{10}$	
Decimal	0.1				5.5
Percentage			60%		

8 Work out these. Write each answer in its simplest form.

  a $3\frac{3}{4} + 2\frac{7}{12}$ **b** $2\frac{8}{9} - 2\frac{1}{2}$

9 Work out $32 \div \frac{4}{5}$

10 Write 4 hours 15 minutes as a mixed number of hours. ....

11 Work out $2\frac{5}{12} + 5\frac{1}{8} - 4\frac{3}{4}$. Write your answer in its simplest form.

12 Work out $\frac{4}{15} \times \frac{5}{16}$

13 Work out $4 \times 3\frac{3}{5}$

14 Work out $8\frac{1}{2} \div \frac{7}{8}$

5.1 Angles and parallel lines

1 Reasoning Work out the angles marked with letters.
Give your reasons.

Guided

$a =$ ......° (vertically opposite angles are equal)

$b = 180° - 30° =$ ......° (angles on a straight line add up to 180°)

$c =$ ....

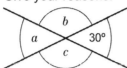

Vertically opposite angles are equal.
The light grey angles are equal.
The dark grey angles are equal.

2 Reasoning Work out the angles marked with letters.
Give reasons for your answers.

Guided

$d = 180° - 50° - 70° =$ ......° (angles on a straight line add up to 180°)

$e =$ ....

$f =$ ....

$g =$ ....

$h =$ ....

$i =$ ....

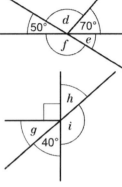

3 Reasoning

a Mark the two pairs of alternate angles.
Use a different colour for each pair.

b Mark the four pairs of corresponding angles.
Use a different colour for each pair.

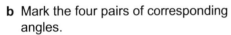

The light grey angles are **alternate angles**.
They are on different (alternate) sides of the diagonal line.
The dark grey angles are **corresponding angles**. They are on the same (corresponding) sides of the diagonal line.

4 Reasoning Work out the angles marked with letters.
Give reasons for your answers.

$a =$ ....

$b =$ ....

$c =$ ....

$d =$ ....

$e =$ ....

$f =$ ....

$g =$ ....

$h =$ ....

$i =$ ....

$j =$ ....

$k =$ ....

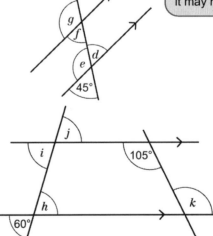

You don't have to work out the angles in the order of the letters but it may help.

Worked example

CHECK Tick each box as your **confidence** in this topic improves.

Need extra help? Go to page 48 and tick the boxes next to Q1, 2 and 3. Then have a go at them once you've finished 5.1–5.4.

1 Complete this table showing the number of lines of symmetry and the order of rotational symmetry of these triangles.

Triangle	Equilateral 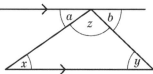	Isosceles	Scalene
number of lines of symmetry			
order of rotational symmetry			

> A **line of symmetry** divides a shape into two halves that fit exactly on top of each other. The **order of rotational symmetry** of a shape is the number of times it exactly fits on top of itself when rotated a full turn.

> If a shape has no line or rotational symmetry, write 'None'.

2 Reasoning   Prove that the angles of a triangle add up to 180°.

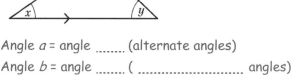

Angle a = angle _____ (alternate angles)

Angle b = angle _____ (_____ angles)

$a + z + b$ = _____° (angles on a _____)

Because $a = x$ and $b = y$, then $a + z + b = x + z + y =$ _____ °

This proves that the angles in a triangle add up to _____ °

> Showing that a rule works for a few values is not enough. You need to **prove** it works for *all* values. A **proof** uses logical reasoning to show a rule is true. You must always give a reason for each statement that you make.

3 Reasoning   Work out the size of angle x.
Give a reason for your answer.

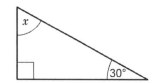

> $x = \boxed{}$ (angles in a triangle add up to $\boxed{}$°)

4 Reasoning   Work out the angles marked with letters.
Give a reason for each step.

a
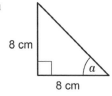

b

Worked example

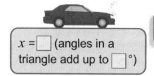

Strategy hint
Explain how you know each triangle is isosceles. Next, identify the two equal angles.

5 Work out the angles marked with letters.
Give reasons for your answers.

6 Reasoning   Prove that an exterior angle of a triangle is equal to the sum of the opposite interior angles.
The exterior angle e is opposite the two interior angles y and z.
Complete this proof.

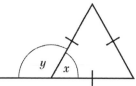

> An **interior angle** is inside a shape.
> An **exterior angle** is outside the shape on a straight line with the interior angle.

$e + x =$ _____° because they lie on a _____.

$x + y + z =$ _____° because the angles in a triangle sum to _____°.

This proves that $e =$ _____

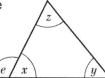

exterior   opposite interior angles

CHECK   Tick each box as your **confidence** in this topic improves.

Need extra help? Go to pages 48–49 and tick the boxes next to Q4, 6 and 7. Then have a go at them once you've finished 5.1–5.4.

45

1 Complete this table showing the number of lines of symmetry and the order of rotational symmetry of these quadrilaterals.

Quadrilateral	Square	Rectangle	Parallelogram	Rhombus	Kite	Arrowhead	Trapezium	Isosceles trapezium
			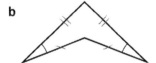					
number of lines of symmetry								
order of rotational symmetry								

2 On each shape below:

- Mark equal sides with dashes. Use double dashes for a second pair of equal sides.

- Mark equal angles with arcs. Use double arcs for a second pair of equal angles.

- Mark right angles.

- Mark parallel sides with arrows. Use double arrows for a second pair of parallel sides.

Guided

a   **b**    **c**

Use line and rotational symmetry to find equal sides and angles.

d 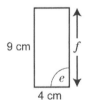   **e** 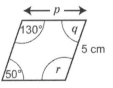   **f** 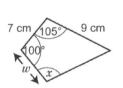   **g**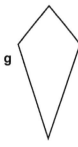

3 Work out the angles and sides marked with letters.

a

9 cm, f, e, 4 cm

rectangle

b

p, 130°, q, 5 cm, 50°, r

rhombus

c

7 cm, 105°, 9 cm, 100°, w, x

kite

d

12 cm, b, 130°, 5 cm, c, 50°, a, 20 cm

isosceles trapezium

------------------------------ --------------------------- ----------------------------- -----------------------------

------------------------------ --------------------------- ----------------------------- -----------------------------

--------------------------- -----------------------------

4 Work out angle a in the quadrilateral.
Give your reason.

30°, a, 70°, 130°

Angles in a quadrilateral sum to 360°.

CHECK   Tick each box as your **confidence** in this topic improves.

Need extra help? Go to page 49 and tick the boxes next to Q5 and 8. Then have a go at them once you've finished 5.1–5.4.

46

5.4 Polygons

A polygon is a closed shape with straight sides. In a regular polygon, the sides and angles are all equal.
Every polygon has exterior angles, e, and interior angles, i.

Equilateral triangle	Square	Regular pentagon	Regular hexagon	Regular polygon of n sides
			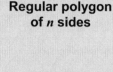	
$3e = 360°$	$4e = 360°$	$5e = 360°$	$6e = 360°$	$ne = 360°$
$3i = 180°$	$4i = 360°$	$5i = 540°$	$6i = 720°$	$ni = 180° \times (n - 2)$

1 Problem-solving   The sum of the interior angles of a polygon is 1260°.
Work out how many sides it has.

  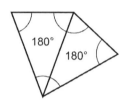 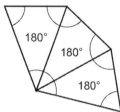

> 3 sides = 180°, 4 sides = 2 × 180 = 360°, 5 sides = 3 × 180 = 540°, ... sides = ... × 180 = 1260°

2 Work out the interior angle of a regular pentagon.

> $S = 180(n - 2) = 180(5 - 2) = 180 \times 3 = 540°$
>
> There are 5 equal interior angles, so each interior angle = ... ÷ .... = ... °

> **Sum of interior angles of an n-sided polygon**
> $S = (n - 2) \times 180°$

3 Reasoning

  a What is the sum of the exterior angles of a regular decagon? ....

  b Work out the size of one of its exterior angles.   360 ÷ .... = ... °

  c Work out the size of one of its interior angles. ....

> A decagon has 10 sides.

4 Problem-solving   The exterior angle of a regular polygon is 18°.

  a Work out the interior angle. ....

  b How many sides does the polygon have? ....

> ☐ × 18° = ☐°

5 A regular polygon has 60 sides. Work out the size of its

  a exterior angle

  b interior angle.

> **Worked example**
>

CHECK   Tick each box as your **confidence** in this topic improves.

Need extra help? Go to page 49 and tick the boxes next to Q9, 10 and 11. Then have a go at them once you've finished 5.1–5.4.

47

5 Strengthen

Angles and parallel lines

☐ **1** Work out the angles marked with letters.
Choose one of these reasons for each answer.

- **S** Angles on a straight line add up to 180° (S).
- **P** Angles at a point add up to 360° (P).
- **V** Vertically opposite angles are equal (V).

a

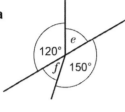

b

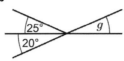

c

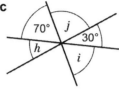

....

....

....

....

....

....

☐ **2 a** Look for a Z-shape in the diagram.

Mark a pair of alternate angles with the letter a.

b Is there another pair of alternate

angles? ....
If so, mark them with the letter b.

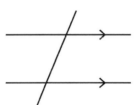

When a line crosses two parallel lines it creates a 'Z' shape.
Inside the Z shape are **alternate angles**.
Alternate angles are equal.

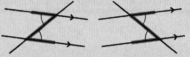

Alternate angles are on different (alternate) sides of the diagonal line.

☐ **3 a** Look for an F-shape in the diagram.
Mark a pair of corresponding angles with the letter c.

b Is there another pair of corresponding

angles? ....
If so, mark them with the letter d.

c Are there any other pairs of

corresponding angles? ....

How many pairs of corresponding angles

are there altogether? ....

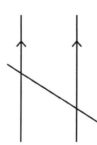

When a line crosses two parallel lines it creates an 'F' shape.
There are **corresponding angles** on an F shape. Corresponding angles are equal.

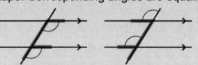

Corresponding angles are on the same (corresponding) side of the diagonal line.

Triangles and quadrilaterals

☐ **4** Work out the angles marked with letters.
Give a reason for each answer.

a

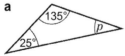

b

The angles in a triangle add up to 180°. Start with 180° and subtract the other angles.

$p = 180 - 135 - $ .... $ = $ .... $°$
(angles in triangle sum to .... °)

☐ **5** Work out angle x for each quadrilateral.

a

x ....

b

x ....

In part **a**, start with
$x =$
$360 - 100 - \square - \square$
$= \square °$
(angle sum of a quadrilateral)

6 All of these triangles are isosceles.
Work out the angles marked with letters.
Give a reason for each answer.

> The two angles at the base of the equal sides of an isosceles triangle are equal.

a

b

c

....

....

....

....

....

....

7 a Which is the exterior angle, g or h? ....

b Work out angle g. Give a reason for your answer.

c Work out angle h. Give a reason for your answer.

8 Work out the angles marked with letters.

$d =$ ....° (opposite angles of a parallelogram)

$e =$ ....° (alternate angles)

$f =$ ....° (angle sum of a triangle)

Interior and exterior angles

9 Follow these steps to find the angle sum of a polygon.

1 Sketch the polygon.

2 Hold your pencil on one vertex.

3 Draw lines to the other vertices.

4 Write 180° in each triangle.

5 Work out the total, e.g. 4 × 180° = ...°

Use this method to find the angle sums of each polygon in the table.

Polygon	Angle sum
square	
pentagon	
hexagon	4 × 180 = ...°
heptagon	
octagon	

10 Salem measured the exterior angles of this hexagon and added them together. Explain how you know her measurements are wrong.

> What should the exterior angles add up to?

11 Problem-solving The exterior angle of a regular polygon is 20°.

a How many exterior angles does the polygon have? ....

b How many sides does the polygon have? ....

> The exterior angles add up to 360°.
> ☐ × 20° = 360°

1 **Problem-solving** This pattern is made up of three identical grey isosceles triangular tiles and three identical white isosceles triangular tiles.

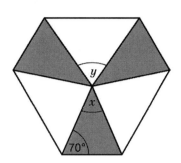

  a Work out angle x. ....

  b Work out angle y. Show your working.

2 **Real** The diagram shows a ship S and a port P on a map. The arrows both point to north. They are parallel. Work out the angle marked a.

Extend the line SP.

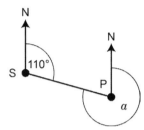

3 **Reasoning** Work out all of the other angles.
ABCD is a rhombus.
DEF is a straight line.
Angle BCD = 70°
Angle AED = 80°
Give reasons for your answers.

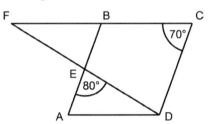

Mark any parallel lines. Write in each angle as you work it out. Describe the angles using 3 letters.

You can describe a shape using the letters at its **vertices** (the plural of **vertex**).
This angle is called angle ABC or ∠ABC.

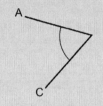

4 **Reasoning** Show that the sum of the interior angles of an icosagon (20-sided shape) is 3240°.

'Show that' means work out the answer and show it is the same as the one given.

5 Work out the angle marked a.
Give reasons.

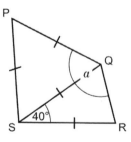

6 Work out the angles marked with letters.
Give reasons for your working.

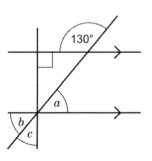

7 In the diagram, angles x and y are called co-interior angles.
Complete this proof that co-interior angles sum to 180°.

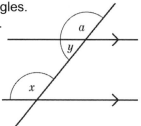

$x =$ .... (............................... angles)

$y =$ .... $-$ .... ° (angles on a straight line)

$x + y =$ .... $+$ .... $=$ .... °

> You must prove that
> $x + y = 180°$.
> Find the expressions
> for x and y and then
> add them together.

8 Work out the angles p, q and r.

a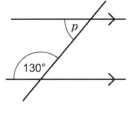

b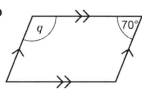

c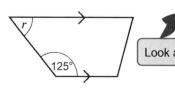

> Look at Q7.

------------------------ ------------------------ ------------------------

9 Reasoning Here are three regular polygons.
Work out the angles marked with letters.
Give a reason for each answer.

> Use line symmetry
> in your calculations.

a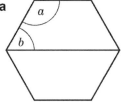

b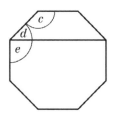

c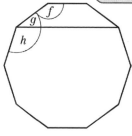

a .... c .... f ....

....

b .... d .... g ....

....

e .... h ....

....

10 A chiliagon is a polygon with 1000 sides. For a regular chiliagon, work out

  a the exterior angle   **b** the interior angle.

11 Work out the angle, x, at the centre of each regular polygon.

> Angle at the centre of an
> n-sided regular polygon $= \dfrac{360°}{n}$

a

b

c

$x = \dfrac{360°}{5} =$ ....° $\quad x = \dfrac{360°}{.....} =$ ....°

----

12 Reasoning The diagram shows
a polygon in the shape of a star.
Angle x is 30°. Work out angle y.

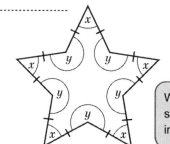

> Work out the
> sum of the
> interior angles.

PROGRESS BAR Colour in the progress bar as you get questions correct. Then fill in the progression chart on pages 107-109.

1 Work out the angles marked with letters. Give a reason for each answer.

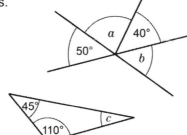

2 Work out angle c.

3 The diagram shows a parallelogram.

a Mark any equal sides, equal angles and parallel lines.

b How many lines of symmetry does a parallelogram have? ....

c Describe the rotational symmetry of a parallelogram.

4 Work out angle d.

5 A quadrilateral has two pairs of equal sides, one pair of equal angles, one line of symmetry and rotational symmetry of order 1. What is its name? ....

6 Work out the angles marked with letters. Give a reason for each answer.

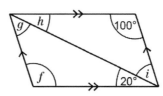

7 The diagram shows the exterior angles of a polygon.

a Work out angle j. ....

b Work out the sum of the interior angles.

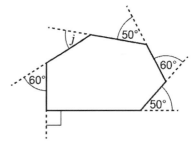

8 Work out angle k. Give a reason for your answer.

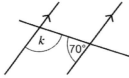

9 a Work out the exterior angle of a regular 36-sided polygon. ....

b Work out the interior angle of a regular 36-sided polygon. ....

10 A regular polygon has an exterior angle of 30°. How many sides does the polygon have? ....

6.1 Ordering decimals

1 Write these decimals in order from smallest to largest.

2.6, 2.39, 2.08

H	T	U	.	$\frac{1}{10}$	$\frac{1}{100}$	$\frac{1}{1000}$
		2	.	6	0	
		2	.	3	9	
		2	.	0	8	

On a place value table, the numbers look like this. Write a **zero place holder** when ordering decimals with different numbers of decimal places.

Digits after the decimal point are fractions.
$0.1 = \frac{1}{10}$
$0.01 = \frac{1}{100}$
$0.001 = \frac{1}{1000}$

2.08, ...

The units are all 2.
$\frac{8}{100}$ is the smallest fraction and $\frac{60}{100}$ is the largest.

2 Write these decimals in order from smallest to largest.

a 0.1, 0.001, 0.01

0.100, 0.001, 0.010 —— Write as decimals with the same number of decimal places.

0.001, ...

b 0.05, 0.5, 0.005

3 Reasoning Ludger says, '1.4 is smaller than 1.25 because 4 is smaller than 25.' Is Ludger correct? Explain.

Ascending means increasing in value from low to high.

4 Write these decimals in ascending order.

a 0.515, 0.55, 0.509 ....

b 25.7635, 25.8, 25.81, 25.764 ....

c −0.805, −0.884, −0.8, −0.85, −0.88 ....

d −1.95, −1.991, −1.97, −1.907, −1.99 ....

Descending means decreasing in value from large to small.

5 Write these decimals in descending order.

a 9.4516, 9.47, 9.4106, 9.416, 9.446 ....

b 77.339, 77.3933, 77.933, 77.9, 77.39 ....

c −5.2, −5.02, −5.145, −5.323 ....

d −6.66, −6.63, −6.663, −6.603, −6.636 ....

6 STEM The bulletproof glass in a car needs to measure between 5.795 cm and 5.805 cm in thickness. The thicknesses of five sheets of glass are

A 5.85 cm, B 5.79 cm, C 5.797 cm, D 5.8 cm, E 5.7955 cm

Which of these sheets are acceptable?

7 Write < or > between each pair of numbers.

a 7.3 .... 7.7
b 4.2 .... 4.17
c 42.106 .... 42.007
d −0.7 .... −0.64
e −4.05 .... −4.044
f −5.1 .... −6.11

CHECK — Tick each box as your **confidence** in this topic improves.

Need extra help? Go to page 60 and tick the box next to Q1. Then have a go at it once you've finished 6.1–6.7.

1 Round these numbers to one decimal place.

a 4.72 = 4.7   **b** 8.44 ....

| 2 is less than 5 so round down. |

> To round a decimal to one decimal place (1 d.p.), look at the digit in the second decimal place. If the digit is less than 5, round down. If the digit is 5 or more, round up. Write the number in the first decimal place, even if it is 0.

c 82.96 ....   **d** 56.75 ....

2 Real Alistair scores 17, 16, 17 and 25 runs in his first four innings of 2014.
Calculate his mean score. Round your answer to 1 decimal place.

3 Problem-solving Elaine writes an answer of 8.7 correct to 1 decimal place.

What could her number have been, correct to 2 decimal places? ....

4 Round these numbers to 2 decimal places.

a 12.368 = 12.37 ——— | 8 is more than 5 so round up. |

> To round to two decimal places (2 d.p.), look at the digit in the third decimal place.

b 48.456 ....   **c** 30.303 ....   **d** 8.997 ....

5 Use a calculator to write these fractions as decimals correct to 2 d.p.

a $\frac{1}{7}$ ....   **b** $\frac{1}{8}$ ....   **c** $\frac{1}{9}$ ....

| Work out 1 ÷ 7 |

6 Reasoning Joanne says that 32.999 rounded to 2 decimal places is 33.

a Explain why Joanne is wrong. ....

b What is the correct answer? ....

7 Finance Chloe buys a pack of five dog chews for £1.99.
How much does each dog chew cost?
Round your answer to the nearest penny.

8 $\sqrt{15} = 3.872983346...$

> To round a decimal to 3 decimal places, look at the digit in the fourth decimal place.

Round this number to 3 decimal places. ....

9 Problem-solving Emma writes down an answer of 7.48 correct to 2 decimal places.
Circle the two which could have been her unrounded answer?

7.475   7.485   7.484   7.4727

10 Problem-solving Write down a number with 3 decimal places that would round to

a 6 to the nearest whole number and 5.7 to the nearest tenth ....

b 5.5 to the nearest tenth and 5.55 to the nearest hundredth. ....

CHECK   Tick each box as your **confidence** in this topic improves.

Need extra help? Go to page 60 and tick the boxes next to Q2 and 3. Then have a go at them once you've finished 6.1–6.7.

6.3 Adding and subtracting decimals

1 Work out

   a 5 – 0.7 ....

   b 8 – 0.2 ....

   c 10 – 4.56 ....

   d 100 – 9.99 ....

Count up.

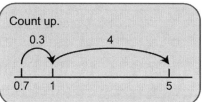

2 Work out

   a 4.65 + 1.73

   b 6.08 + 4.8

Worked example

3 **Reasoning** Josh says, '12.25 + 7.3 = 19.28, because 12 + 7 = 19 and 25 + 3 = 28.'
Explain why Josh is wrong.

Estimate by rounding the values to the nearest whole number to do the calculation.

4 Work out these. Use an estimate to check your answer.

   a 7.84 – 3.41

   b 33.33 – 8.8

5 **Real / Problem-solving / Finance** Andy orders:

Pizza	£7.95
Apple pie	£3.99
Spring water	£1.55

How much change does Andy get from £20? ....
Use an estimate to check your answer.

6 **Real** Karen has a 4.25 m length of tubing. She saws off a piece 2.87 m long.
How long is the remaining tubing?

7 Work out these using the column method.

   a 9.3 + 2.8 – 5.21

```
  9.3          12.10
+ 2.8        -  5.21
12₁.1
```

Line up the units, tenths and hundredths.

   b 4.75 + 5.57 – 8.8

You can use a zero place holder when subtracting decimals with different numbers of decimal places.

Check: 9.3 ≈ 9, 2.8 ≈ 3, 5.21 ≈ 5.
9 + 3 – 5 = 7

8 The population of England was 45 370 530 in 1911.
In 2011 it was 53 107 200. Estimate the population increase.

Write the population as millions to 1 d.p.

CHECK   Tick each box as your **confidence** in this topic improves.

Need extra help? Go to page 60 and tick the boxes next to Q4, 5 and 6. Then have a go at them once you've finished 6.1–6.7.

6.4 Multiplying decimals

1 Use the column method to work out these. Use an estimate to check your answers.

a 2.8 × 9

b 4.15 × 8

Estimate: 2.8 ≈ 3, 3 × 9 = 27

```
    2 8
×     9
  2 5 2
    7
```

Ignore the decimal point and work out 28 × 9

2.8 × 9 = 25.2

Use your estimate to see where to put the decimal point.

You can use the column method to multiply a decimal by a whole number.

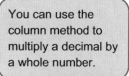

Worked example

2 Real / Finance It costs £2.25 to post a parcel. How much does it cost to post 7 parcels?

3 Work out

Your answer will have the digits 4 and 5. Where do you put the decimal point?

a 5 × 9 _____   **b** 5 × 0.9 _____   **c** 0.5 × 9 _____

d 5 × 0.09 _____   **e** 50 × 0.9 _____   **f** 0.05 × 0.09 _____

4 Use the multiplication facts given to work out the answers.

a 51 × 10 = 510   Work out **i** 51 × 0.1 _____   **ii** 51 ÷ 10 _____

b 87 × 10 = 870   Work out **i** 87 × 0.1 _____   **ii** 87 ÷ 10 _____

5 a Work out

i 63 × 1 _____   **ii** 63 × 0.1 _____   **iii** 63 × 0.01 _____

b Reasoning What division calculation is equivalent to × 0.01? _____

6 Work out these. Check your answer using an estimate.

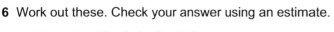

a 23 × 2.4 = 20 × 2.4 + 3 × 2.4 = _____ + _____ = _____

b 41 × 3.2 _____

You can use **partitioning** to work out decimal multiplications. You can check your answer using an estimate.

7 Real / Finance Ahmed changes £50 to dollars. The exchange rate is £1 = $1.60. How many dollars does he get?

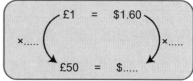

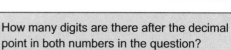

8 Use the fact 0.47 × 2.8 = 1.316 to calculate

How many digits are there after the decimal point in both numbers in the question?

a 0.047 × 2.8 _____

b 4.7 × 28 _____

c 470 × 0.028 _____

d Write down two other multiplications that will have an answer of 1.316.

CHECK   Tick each box as your **confidence** in this topic improves.

Need extra help? Go to pages 60 and 61 and tick the boxes next to Q7–10. Then have a go at them once you've finished 6.1–6.7.

56

6.5 Dividing decimals

1 Work out

a $64.2 \div 3$

$$\begin{array}{r} 2\,1.\ 4 \\ 3\overline{)6\,4.\,{}^12} \end{array} \quad 64.2 \div 3 = 21.4$$

> First write the decimal point for the answer above the decimal point in the question. Then divide as normal, starting from the left.

> You can use short or long division to divide a decimal by a whole number.

b $75.5 \div 5$

c $86.8 \div 7$

2 Work out

a $8 \div 0.1$

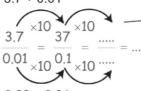

$$\frac{8}{0.1} \overset{\times 10}{\underset{\times 10}{=}} \frac{80}{1} = 80 \quad 8 \div 0.1 = 80$$

b $3.7 \div 0.01$

$$\frac{3.7}{0.01} \overset{\times 10}{\underset{\times 10}{=}} \frac{37}{0.1} \overset{\times 10}{\underset{\times 10}{=}} \frac{.....}{.....} = ...$$

> Multiply the numerator and denominator by 10 until you have a whole number in the denominator.

c $0.4 \div 0.1$

d $0.22 \div 0.01$

3 Work out

a $8 \div 0.4$

b $50 \div 0.2$

> Use the same method as in Q2.

c $300 \div 0.05$

d $24 \div 0.06$

4 Work out.

a i $48 \div 12$ ....   **ii** $4.8 \div 1.2$ ....

b i $36 \div 9$ ....   **ii** $3.6 \div 0.9$ ....

c i $284 \div 4$ ....   **ii** $2.84 \div 0.04$ ....

d i $246 \div 8 = 30.75$ **ii** $2.46 \div 0.08$ ....

> **Worked example**

5 Work out

a $0.8 \div 0.4$ ....   **b** $0.21 \div 0.7$ ....

c $0.04 \div 0.02$ ....   **d** $0.32 \div 0.08$ ....

6 Continue the pattern to work out the answers.

a $5312 \div 83 = 64$ $5312 \div 8.3 = 640$ $5312 \div 0.83 = $ .... $5312 \div 0.083 = $ ....

b $925 \div 37 = 25$ $92.5 \div 37 = $ .... $9.25 \div 37 = $ .... $0.925 \div 37 = $ ....

7 $3.8 \times 62 = 235.6$

> Use number patterns similar to Q6 to help.

Use this multiplication fact to work out

a $235.6 \div 62$ ....   **b** $235.6 \div 3.8$ ....   **c** $235.6 \div 6.2$ ....

d $23.56 \div 62$ ....   **e** $235.6 \div 38$ ....   **f** $23.56 \div 3.8$ ....

CHECK   Tick each box as your **confidence** in this topic improves.

Need extra help? Go to page 61 and tick the boxes next to Q11 and 12. Then have a go at them once you've finished 6.1–6.7.

1 Complete the table by finding the missing fractions, decimals or percentages.

Fraction				$\frac{3}{4}$	$\frac{4}{5}$		
Decimal	0.5			0.1		1.9	
Percentage		25%	20%				250%

2 Convert these decimals to percentages.

  a 0.22 ....   **b** 0.03 ....   **c** 4.04 ....

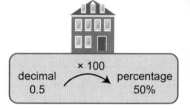

decimal × 100 → percentage
0.5 → 50%

3 Convert these percentages to decimals.

  a 17% ....   **b** 345% ....   **c** 3.8% ....

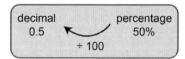

decimal ← percentage
0.5 ÷ 100 → 50%

4 Write each time as a decimal number of hours.

  a 2 h 45 min ....   **b** 5 h 24 min ....

> Write as a mixed number first.

5 Write these decimals as fractions. Simplify the fractions where possible.

  a $0.4 = \frac{4}{10} = \frac{....}{....}$ **b** $0.44 = \frac{44}{100} = \frac{....}{....}$ **c** 1.35 ....

 Guided

Worked example

6 Match each fraction to its recurring decimal.

  $\frac{1}{6}$ $\frac{5}{9}$ $\frac{5}{11}$ $\frac{7}{12}$ $\frac{14}{27}$

  $0.1\dot{6}$ $0.\dot{4}\dot{5}$ $0.5\dot{1}\dot{8}$ $0.5\dot{8}\dot{3}$

> In a **recurring decimal,** a dot over the beginning and end of a sequence shows it recurs. For example 0.111111111 is $0.\dot{1}$ and 4.185185185 is $4.\dot{1}8\dot{5}$.

7 Write these recurring decimals using dots.

  a 0.888... ....   **b** 0.275275… ....   **c** 0.005222... ....

8 Put these quantities in ascending order.

  $\frac{2}{3}$ 66%   0.65   6.75% $\frac{7}{10}$ 0.608

> **Strategy hint**
> Convert all the values to decimals first.

9 Convert these percentages to fractions. Give your answer in its simplest form.

  a 17% ....   **b** 2% ....   **c** 85% ....

> Per cent means out of 100.
>
> $17\% = \frac{\square}{\square}$

10 Jo's test marks are given as proportions. Write each one as a percentage. Round your answer to 1 d.p. where necessary.

  a Maths: 27 out of 40 ....

  b ICT: 33 out of 48 ....

  c English: 24 out of 31 ....

  d In which test did Jo do best? ....

> Write as a fraction, then a decimal, then a percentage.

CHECK   Tick each box as your **confidence** in this topic improves.

Need extra help? Go to page 61 and tick the boxes next to Q13 and 14. Then have a go at them once you've finished 6.1–6.7.

6.7 FINANCE: Working with percentages

1 Finance Work out

  a 31% of £210 ....

  b 45% of £110 ....

> Work out 10% first.
> 31% = 30% + 1%

2 Finance Elise puts £250 into a savings account.
The account pays 3% interest per year.
How much money is in the account after 1 year?

> First work out 3% of £250.
> Then add the answer to £250.

3 Problem-solving / Finance Ali wants to buy a new bike.
He sees the same bike on sale at two different shops.

Which shop should he buy it from? ....

4 Finance Use a calculator to work out 4.7% of £627.50.

  4.7% = 4.7 ÷ 100 = ... ⸺ First convert 4.7% to a decimal.

  4.7% of £627.50 = ... × £627.50 = £........

  Answer: £ ....

> You can use a **multiplier** to work out a percentage, by using the decimal equivalent of the percentage.

> Always round money to the nearest penny.

5 Finance / Problem-solving

  a Work out 25% of £500. ....

  b Add your answer to part **a** to £500. ....

  c Work out £500 × 1.25. ....

  d What do you notice about your answers to parts **b** and **c**? ....

  e Complete the sentences.

    i To increase by 25%, multiply by ....   **ii** To increase by 60%, multiply by ....

6 Write down the multiplier for each percentage increase or decrease.

  a 28% increase ....

  b 8% decrease ....

  c 19.9% decrease ....

> Decrease by 8%
> = 100% − 8%
> = ☐ %

7 Finance Ulma and her dad bought a surfboard.
Ulma paid 40% of the cost of the surfboard. She paid £120.
How much did the surfboard cost in total?

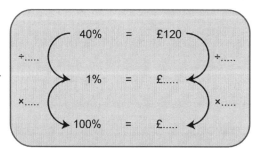

CHECK Tick each box as your **confidence** in this topic improves.

Need extra help? Go to page 61 and tick the boxes next to Q15, 16 and 17. Then have a go at them once you've finished 6.1–6.7.

6 Strengthen

Ordering and rounding decimals

1 Write these numbers in order from smallest to largest.

a 8.3, 9.5, 9.2, 8.4 ....

b 0.55, 0.006, 0.606, 0.055, 0.06 ....

Use the number line to help you.

0.752

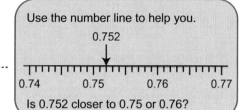

Is 0.752 closer to 0.75 or 0.76?

2 Round each number to 2 decimal places.

a 0.752 ....

b 0.768 ....

c 0.7455 ....

d 0.7549 ....

3 Work out, to the nearest penny, £4.30 ÷ 3 ....

Add and subtract decimals

4 Work out these. Use an estimate to check your answers.

a 27 − 2.3 = 24. ....

b 100 − 15.1 ....

First subtract the whole number.
Then subtract the decimal.

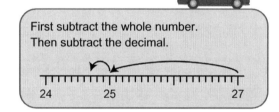

5 Work out these. Use an estimate to check your answers.

a 6.7 + 1.43

b 8.55 + 4.6

6. 7 0 — Write a zero to make the calculation easier.
+ 1. 4 3

When using the column method, always line up the decimal points.

6 Work out these. Use an estimate to check your answers.

a 3.7 − 0.22

b 25.5 − 2.42

c 7.3 − 0.898

Write a zero to make the calculation easier.

Worked example

Multiply and divide decimals

7 Work out these multiplications. Use an estimate to check your answers.

a 2.6 × 2

26 × 2 = 52, so 2.6 × 2 = ...

Use a number pattern.

b 21.5 × 3

c 10.13 × 4

8 Use a mental method and the multiplication facts you know to work out

a 8 × 0.3 ....

b 70 × 0.2 ....

c 0.04 × 6 ....

d 30 × 0.06 ....

Use a number pattern.
8 × 3 = 24, 8 × 0.3 = ☐

9 Work out

    a 0.5 × 0.5

> Use a number pattern.

    5 × 5 = 25, 5 × 0.5 = 2.5, 0.5 × 0.5 = ...

    b 0.04 × 0.7 ....   **c** 0.08 × 0.05........................

10 Work out

    a 5.2 × 0.41   **b** 0.32 × 2.12

> Use a pattern to work out 5.2 × 0.41
>
> $$\begin{array}{r} 52 \\ \times\ 41 \\ \hline \\ \hline \end{array}$$

11 Work out

    a 42.3 ÷ 3   **b** 36.15 ÷ 5

> $3\overline{)423}$
> 423 ÷ 3 = ☐
> 42.3 ÷ 3 = ☐

12 Work out

    a 8 ÷ 0.2   **b** 27 ÷ 0.9

> Use a number pattern.
> **a** 8 ÷ 2, 8 ÷ 0.2
> **d** 6 ÷ 3, 0.6 ÷ 3, 0.6 ÷ 0.3, 0.6 ÷ 0.03

    c 42 ÷ 0.06   **d** 0.6 ÷ 0.03

Fractions, decimals and percentages

13 Complete these number lines showing percentages, decimals and fractions.
Write each fraction in its simplest form.

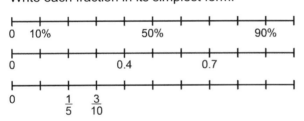

> First complete the percentages number line, then the decimals, then the fractions. Write the fractions as tenths and simplify.

14 Which card does not have an equivalent card?

1.33   140% $\frac{2}{3}$ $0.\dot{6}$ $\frac{4}{3}$ 1.25   133.33...%   1.4 $\frac{5}{4}$

15 Work out

    a 1% of 40 = 40 ÷ 100 = 0.4   **b** 11% of 40 = 0.4 × 11 = ...

    c 1% of £140 ....   **d** 29% of £140 ....

> $1\% = \frac{1}{100}$
> 1% of 40 = ...
> ×11   ×11
> 11% of 40 = ...

16 a Increase £50 by 40%.   **b** Decrease 80 m*l* by 35%.

> £50
> 40%
> .....

17 80% of an amount is 48.
Work out the original amount.

> 48
> 80%   20%
> 1% = 48 ÷ 80

6 Extend

1 Problem-solving In a canteen each person selected one pudding.

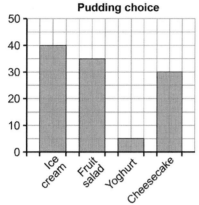

Pudding choice

a How many puddings were selected? 40 + 35 + 5 + 30 = ...

b What percentage selected cheesecake, rounded to 1 d.p.?

$\dfrac{30}{.....}$ × 100 = ...

c What percentage selected ice cream, rounded to 1 d.p.? ....

d Write your answers to parts **b** and **c** as a recurring decimal. ....

2 Problem-solving John rounded a number with two decimal places and got the answer 8.3.

a What is the smallest number John could have rounded up to 8.3? ....

b What is the largest number John could have rounded down to 8.3? ....

3 Billy's height was measured on his 13th birthday. He is now taller than 150 cm. His height has increased by 10% since his 12th birthday.

Write a possible height for Billy on his 12th birthday. ....

> Try some different heights.

4 Problem-solving In an experiment, two identical 1.4 m long metal bars are at room temperature.
The first bar is cooled and shrinks by 1%.
The second bar is heated and expands by 2%.
Work out the range of the metal bars' lengths.

5 8.7 × 43 = 374.1

Use this number fact to work out these.

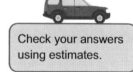

> Check your answers using estimates.

a 0.87 × 43 ....
b 0.87 × 4.3 ....

c 0.0087 × 430 ....
d 374.1 ÷ 43 ....

e 374.1 ÷ 8.7 ....
f 37.41 ÷ 4.3 ....

6 $\dfrac{46}{99} = 0.\overset{\bullet}{4}\overset{\bullet}{6}$ $\dfrac{47}{99} = 0.\overset{\bullet}{4}\overset{\bullet}{7}$

Use these number facts to write these fractions as recurring decimals.

a $\dfrac{48}{99}$ ....
b $\dfrac{5}{99}$ ....
c $\dfrac{66}{99}$ ....

d Write $\dfrac{567}{999}$ as a recurring decimal. ....

Check your answer using a calculator.

7 Finance Mark wants to buy a new racing bike. The price is £1299.95.
He can pay in 12 equal monthly payments.

   a How much would he pay per month? ....

He is offered a 15% discount for paying all at once.

   b How much will he save by choosing this option? ....

   c How much will he pay if he chooses this option? ....

8 Carla says, '0.1 × 0.3 × −0.5 = −0.15 because 1 × 3 × −5 = −15.'
Explain why Carla is wrong. What is the correct answer?

9 Finance Rita invested £1000. She earned 3% simple interest per year.

   a How much interest will Rita have after 1 year?

   b How much money will Rita have altogether after 39 months?

Write 39 months in years and months. Then convert this to a decimal number of years.

10 Finance / Problem-solving Jasmine invested £300. She earned simple interest over 3 years.
At the end of 3 years, her investment was worth £345. It increased by the same amount every year.
What interest rate did she receive?

11 Write these in ascending order.

   5% $\frac{4}{90}$ 0.5 $\frac{5}{99}$ 4.52% $\frac{9}{200}$

12 Reasoning Write < or > between each pair of numbers.

   a **i** 0.5 .... 0.2

      ii −0.5 .... −0.2

   b **i** −0.63 .... −0.45

      ii 0.63 .... 0.45

   c If $x > y$, then $-x$ .... $-y$.

Use your answers to parts **a** and **b** to answer part **c**.

13 Problem-solving Phil is thinking of a number.
Write down a possible value for Phil's number at each step.

   a His number has 3 digits after the decimal point. ....

   b His number rounds to 51 to the nearest whole number. ....

   c His number rounds to 50.7 to the nearest tenth. ....

   d His number rounds to 50.73 to the nearest hundredth. ....

6 Unit test

> **PROGRESS BAR** Colour in the progress bar as you get questions correct.
> Then fill in the progression chart on pages 107-109.

1 a Work out 10% of 45. ....

b Work out 1% of 45. ....

c Use your answers to parts **a** and **b** to work out 33% of 45.

2 A roll of wallpaper is 10.5 m.
Eva cuts off a piece 2.65 m long.
How long is the remaining piece?

3 Complete this table of fractions, decimals and percentages.
Write all fractions in their simplest form.

Fraction	$\frac{7}{10}$				$1\frac{2}{3}$
Decimal		0.75		1.4	
Percentage			60%		

4 Use the fact that 38 × 3.03 = 115.14 to work out

a 3.8 × 3.03 .... **b** 38 × 303 .... **c** 115.14 ÷ 3.8 ....

5 Write these decimals in ascending order: 1.38, 1.08, 1.8, 1.183, 1.083 ....

6 Round 12.577 to 2 decimal places. ....

7 Work out

a 4 × 0.8 .... **b** 0.03 × 70 .... **c** 0.28 ÷ 0.04 ....

8 The same 3D TV is on sale in two different shops.

a What is the cost of the 3D TV in Tom's TVs?

b What is the cost of the 3D TV in TV4U?

9 25% of an amount is 7.5. Work out the original amount.

10 Richard invested £400. He earned 3% simple interest.

a How much money will Richard have after 1 year?

b How much money will Richard have after 27 months?

11 Write < or > for this pair of numbers. −8.23 .... −8.32

1 Use the inverse function to find each missing input.

a

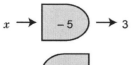

..... → | × 3 | → 21

← ⊂ ← 21

b

..... → | − 5 | → 12

← ⊂ ← 12

> A function is a rule. The function +3 adds 3 to a number.
> The inverse function is −3 because it reverses the effect of the function +3.
>
> 2 → | + 3 | → 5
>
> 2 ← ⊂ − 3 ← 5

2 Complete the function machines to solve these equations.

a $x - 5 = 3$

x → | − 5 | → 3

..... ← ⊂ ← 3

$x = $ .....

b $2x = 12$

x → | × 2 | → 12

..... ← ⊂ ← 12

$x = $ .....

> An equation contains an unknown number (a letter) and an '=' sign. To solve an equation means to work out the value of the unknown number.

3 Solve these equations.

a $\dfrac{t}{4} = 8$

$\dfrac{4 \times t}{4} = 4 \times 8$

$t = $ ....

Check: .... $\div 4 = 8$ ✓

b $x + 5 = 19$

> Balance the equation by multiplying both sides by 4.

> Check by replacing t in the equation with your solution.

> Visualise the function machines to decide which inverse to use.
>
> t → | ÷ 4 | → 8
>
> ..... ← ⊂ × 4 ← 8

> In an equation, the expressions on both sides of the equals sign have the same value. You can visualize them on balanced scales.
>
> | $t + 3$ | − | 8 |
> △
>
> To stay balanced, do the same operation to both sides.
>
> | $t + 3 - 3$ | − | $8 - 3$ |
> △
>
> This is called the **balancing method**.

4 a Write an equation for these six angles.

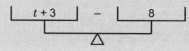

----

b Solve your equation to find the value of t.

> What do the angles on a straight line add up to?

5 Problem-solving / Modelling   Tickets for 2 adults and 5 children to a pantomime come to £54.
An adult ticket costs twice as much as a child ticket.
Work out the price of an adult ticket.

> Use t to stand for the cost of a child ticket.
>
> child tickets   adult tickets
>
> | t | t | t | t | t | $2t$ | $2t$ |
>
> £54

CHECK   Tick each box as your **confidence** in this topic improves.   😟 😐 😊

Need extra help? Go to page 69 and tick the boxes next to Q1–3. Then have a go at them once you've finished 7.1–7.4.

7.2 Solving two-step equations

1 Draw function machines to solve each equation.

a $3x + 2 = 14$ **b** $5p - 1 = 34$ **c** $\frac{d}{3} + 10 = 12$

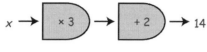

$x \rightarrow \boxed{\times 3} \rightarrow \boxed{+2} \rightarrow 14$

$..... \leftarrow \boxed{.......} \leftarrow \boxed{-2} \leftarrow 14$

$x = ...$

2 Use the balancing method to solve these equations.

a $3x + 5 = 17$ | Balance the equation by subtracting 5 from each side. | **b** $2x - 5 = 11$

$3x + 5 - 5 = 17 - 5$

$3x = 12$ | Balance again by dividing both sides by 3. |

$x = ...$

Check: $3 \times ....+ 5 = 17 \checkmark$

3 STEM Substitute the values given into each formula.
Solve the equation to find the unknown value.

a $y = mx + c$

Find x when $y = 9$, $m = 3$ and $c = -4$.

b $s = ut + \frac{1}{2}at^2$

Work out a when $s = 30$, $u = 4$ and $t = 3$.

4 Solve the equation $-2x + 9 = -3$

Worked example

5 Modelling Koa says, 'I think of a number, multiply it by 4 and add 5. My answer is 49.'

a Write an equation to show Koa's calculation. Use n for the number he thinks of.

b Solve your equation to work out Koa's number.

6 Modelling Work out the sizes of the angles.

a

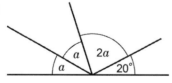

| Work out the value of the letter first. |

b

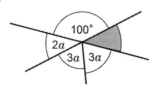

| What do you know about the grey angle? |

CHECK Tick each box as your **confidence** in this topic improves.

Need extra help? Go to page 69 and tick the boxes next to Q4, 5 and 6. Then have a go at them once you've finished 7.1–7.4.

66

7.3 More complex equations

Guided

1 Solve these equations.

a $4x - 1 = 3x + 2$

> You need to end up with $x = \boxed{}$, so start by subtracting $3x$ from both sides, which leaves an x term on the left-hand side and no x term on the right.

$4x - 3x - 1 = 3x - 3x + 2$

$x - 1 = 2$

$x - 1 + 1 = 2 + 1$

> Simplify.

$x = \underline{\ldots\ldots}$

> Add 1 to both sides.

Check: $4 \times \underline{\ldots\ldots} - 1 = \underline{\ldots\ldots}$

$3 \times \underline{\ldots\ldots} + 2 = \underline{\ldots\ldots}$

> Substitute $x = \boxed{}$ into both sides to check they have the same value.

b $8x - 3 = 7x - 1$

> **Worked example**
>
>

c $6t - 4 = 4t + 4$

d $6x = 3(x + 2)$

e $8(x - 6) = 2(x + 6)$ [Expand the brackets first.]

2 Modelling   Deepak says, 'I think of a number, multiply it by 10 and subtract 6. When I start again with the same number, double it and add 12, I get the same answer.'

a Write an expression for each of Deepak's calculations. $\underline{\ldots\ldots\ldots}$ and $\underline{\ldots\ldots\ldots}$

b Write an equation to show that both calculations give the same answer. $\underline{\ldots\ldots\ldots}$

c Solve your equation to find the number Deepak was thinking of.

3 Solve these equations.

a $2x + 5 = 4x - 1$

b $5y + 4 = 2(y + 5)$

c $6(z + 8) = 8(z + 5)$

4 Modelling / Problem-solving   Write an equation and solve it, to find the size of each angle.

a

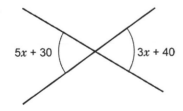

$5x + 30$ $3x + 40$

b

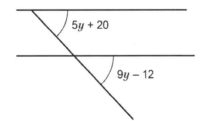

$5y + 20$

$9y - 12$

> What do you know about the two angles?

CHECK   Tick each box as your **confidence** in this topic improves.   😞 😐 🙂

Need extra help? Go to page 70 and tick the boxes next to Q7 and 8. Then have a go at them once you've finished 7.1–7.4.

67

1 Solve these equations.

 Guided

a $x^2 = 64$

$x = \sqrt{64} = \pm$ ....

b $x^3 = 27$

$x = \sqrt[3]{27} =$ ....

c $2x^2 = 18$

In part **c**

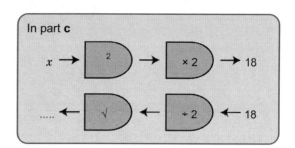

2 Solve these equations using trial and improvement.
Give your answers to 1 decimal place.

 Guided

a $x^3 = 50$

x	x^3	Comment
3	27	too small
4	64	too big
3.5	42.875	too small
3.6	46.656	too small
3.7	50.653	too big

x is between 3.6 and ....
3.7^3 (50.653) is closer to 50
than 3.6^3 (46.656)
so $x =$ .... (1 d.p.)

50 is between the cube
numbers 27 (3^3) and 64 (4^3).
So $\sqrt[3]{50}$ is between 3 and 4.

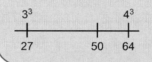

Try the value halfway between
3 and 4. Cube the value.
Decide if it is too big or too
small.

Find two values to 1 d.p. that
x lies between. Decide which
gives the answer closer to 50.

b $x^2 = 56$

3 **Modelling / Problem-solving**   A square tile has area 232 cm^2.
Work out the length of one side, to 1 decimal place.

4 Solve these equations using trial and improvement. Give your answers to 1 decimal place.

a $x^2 - x = 17$ **b** $x^3 + x = 400$

x	$x^2 - x$	Comment

Worked example

CHECK   Tick each box as your **confidence** in this topic improves.

Need extra help? Go to page 71 and tick the boxes next to Q9 and 10. Then have a go at them once you've finished 7.1–7.4.

7 Strengthen

Solving equations

1 Work out the value of each symbol.

Use number facts and times tables.

  a $5 + \diamond = 9$ ....

  b $3 \times \square = 15$ ....

  c $\frac{\triangle}{4} = 2$ ....

2 Solve these equations. Check each answer.

  a $p + 4 = 17$ **b** $21 = 12 + q$ **c** $r - 8 = 10$

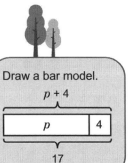

Draw a bar model.

$p + 4$

| p | 4 |

17

3 Solve these equations. Check each answer.

  a $4d = 20$ **b** $3e = -21$ **c** $\frac{f}{10} = 22$

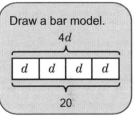

Draw a bar model.

$4d$

| d | d | d | d |

20

4 Solve these equations.

 Guided

  a $5x - 3 = 7$

       Add 3 to both sides.

  $5x = 10$

       Divide both sides by $\square$.

  $x =$ ....

  b $3y + 4 = 16$ **c** $\frac{z}{2} + 3 = 7$

Worked example

5 Solve these equations.

 Guided

  a $20 - 2x = 8$

  $20 = 2x + 8$ Add $2x$ to both sides.

  .... $= 2x$

  $x =$ ....

  b $12 - 4x = 4$ **c** $5 - 3x = 11$

6 Use the formula $W = ax - d$ to find the value of a when $W = 3$, $x = 7$ and $d = 11$.

Substitute in the numbers you know, then solve to work out the value of a.

7 Solve

a $5(x - 2) = 3(x + 2)$

b $4(x + 3) = 6(x + 1)$

Guided

$5x - 10 = 3x + 6$ | Expand the brackets.

.... $- 10 = 6$

Subtract $3x$ from both sides.

.... $=$ ....

$x =$ ....

Writing equations

8 Modelling

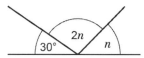

a Write an equation for these angles. ....

b Solve to find n.

c Write down the size of the largest angle. ....

9 Problem-solving / Modelling The diagram shows a rectangle made from two squares.
The area of the rectangle is 242 cm^2.
Work out the length of the rectangle.

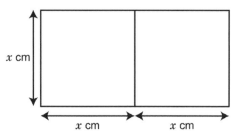

x cm

x cm x cm

Write an equation. Find x, then use this value to find the length of each side.

Trial and improvement

10 Follow these steps to solve $x^2 = 42$ to 1 decimal place.

a Which two square numbers is 42 between? ....

b Complete this number line, using your square numbers from part **a**.

c Fill in the top two rows of the table. Use the values from your number line.

Guided

d Write the value halfway between the first two values of x in line 3. Work out x^2.

e Which two values does x lie between now? Choose a value between them.
Write it in your table and work out x^2.

f Keep trying values of x between 6 and 7.
You should end up with these values:

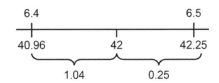

6.4   6.5

40.96   42   42.25

1.04   0.25

x	x^2	Comment
6		too small
	49	

Write down the value that gives x^2 closer to 42. ....

1 Problem-solving   A regular polygon has an interior angle of 135°.
What is the name of the polygon?

Find the exterior angle first.

interior   exterior

$$\text{exterior angle} = \frac{360°}{\text{number of sides}}$$

2 Modelling / Problem-solving   The length of a rectangle is
twice its width.

a Sketch the rectangle.
Label its width w.

Literacy hint
An expression in terms of
w includes the letter w.

What is the length of the rectangle in terms of w? ....

b The perimeter of the rectangle is 30 cm.
Work out the length and the width.

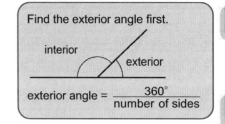

3 Modelling / Problem-solving   Two consecutive integers add to make 165.
What are the two integers?

Guided

1st number = n, 2nd number = $n + 1$

$n + n + 1 = 2n + 1$

$2n + 1 = 165$

Write an expression for each of the
two integers.
Then add your expressions together.

The two integers add to make 165.
Write this as an equation.

Solve your equation to find the value of n.
Write down the two integers.

An **integer** is a whole
number.
Two **consecutive** integers
come one after the other
on a number line.
4 and 5 are consecutive
numbers.
So are 976 and 977.

4 Modelling / Problem-solving   The sum of three consecutive integers is 78.
What are the three integers?

Three **consecutive** integers come
one after the other on a number line.
Three consecutive integers: n, $n + 1$, $n + 2$.

5 Modelling / Real   Madison and Mason are twins. They have a dog called Humpty.
The twins are t years old and are 11 years older than Humpty.

a The total age of all three is 34.

Write an expression for their total age. ....

Humpty's age is $t - 11$.

b Write an equation and solve it to find t.

c How old is Humpty? ....

6 Modelling   Audrey is 4 years younger than her husband.
Their total age is 154.
What are their ages?

7 Modelling   I think of a positive number, square it, subtract 4 and the answer is 60.

  a Write an equation to represent this problem. ....

  b Solve it to find my number.

8 Modelling   A rectangular decking is three times as long as it is wide.
Its area is 33 m^2 to the nearest m^2.

  a Write an equation for the area. ....

  b Solve it to find the width of the decking. Give your answer to 1 decimal place.

9 Continue this table to use trial and improvement to find the solution to $x^3 + x = 60$, to 1 decimal place.

x	$x^3 + x$	Comment
3	30	too small
4	68	too big
3.8		
3.9		

Which of 3.8 or 3.9 gives $x^3 + x$ closer to 60? ....

10 Use trial and improvement to find the solution to $x^3 - x = 130$, to 2 decimal places.

x	$x^3 - x$	Comment

> **PROGRESS BAR** Colour in the progress bar as you get questions correct.
> Then fill in the progression chart on pages 107–109.

1 Solve these equations.

 a $x - 5 = 2$ **b** $3x = 27$ **c** $\frac{x}{4} = 8$

2 Solve these equations.

 a $2x + 4 = 10$ **b** $\frac{x}{4} - 3 = 2$ **c** $2(x + 3) = 22$

3 Work out the size of each angle in this triangle.

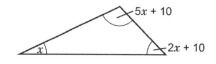

4 Use the formula $A = \frac{1}{2}bh + 2h^2$ to work out the value of b when $h = 10$ and $A = 410$.

5 Solve the equation $4(x + 1) = 2(x + 3)$.

6 The sum of three consecutive numbers is 42. What are the three numbers?

7 Solve $3x^2 = 108$.

8 Use trial and improvement to find the solution to $x^2 - x = 83$, correct to 1 decimal place.

x	$x^2 - x$	Comment

> You need to know these conversions between metric and **imperial** units.
> 1 foot (ft) ≈ 30 cm, 1 mile ≈ 1.6 km, 1 kg ≈ 2.2 pounds (lb), 1 litre ≈ 1.75 pints, 1 gallon ≈ 4.5 litres

1 Complete these.

   a 5 ha = ... m^2

   b .... ha = 55 000 m^2

   c 1.5 t = ... kg

   d .... t = 20 000 kg

> 1 hectare (ha) = 10 000 m^2
> 1 tonne (t) = 1000 kg

2 A farmer has half a hectare to plant fruit trees in.
Each fruit tree must have 25 m^2 to grow.
How many trees can the farmer plant?

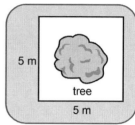

5 m   tree   5 m

3 Problem-solving Gerry buys a 1 kg bag of sugar. On the side of the pack it says,
'Enough for 200 teaspoons of sugar.' Approximately how much sugar is in one teaspoon?

4 Complete these imperial to metric conversions.

   a 10 miles ≈ .... km

   b $\frac{1}{4}$ mile ≈ .... km = ... m

   c 5 ft ≈ .... cm = ... m

   d $\frac{1}{4}$ ft ≈ .... cm

   e 4 lb ≈ .... kg = ... g

   f $\frac{1}{4}$ lb ≈ .... g = ... kg

   g 8 pints ≈ .... litres = ... m*l*

   h $\frac{1}{4}$ pint ≈ .... litres = ... m*l*

   i 3 gallons ≈ .... litres

   j $\frac{1}{4}$ gallon ≈ .... litres = ... m*l*

> 1 mile   × 1.6   1.6 km
> × ......
> 10 miles   ÷ ......   × ......
> ...... km

5 Real / Problem-solving Norman runs between 5 and 10 miles every day.

   a How far does he run in km? ....

The Sahara desert marathon, the 'Marathon des Sables' is 250 km and takes 6 days.

   b Norman trains for it by running twice as far as normal each day. Will he be able to finish the race?

6 Real An airline has a maximum size for carry-on luggage of 56 cm × 45 cm × 25 cm.
Can you carry on a bag with dimensions 24 in × 15 in × 10 in?

> 1 inch ≈ 2.5 cm

CHECK Tick each box as your **confidence** in this topic improves.

Need extra help? Go to page 80 and tick the box next to Q1. Then have a go at it once you've finished 8.1–8.6.

8.2 Writing ratios

1 Real To make concrete to repair a path, you mix 2 buckets of cement with 7 buckets of sand.
The ratio of cement to sand is 2 : 7
I have 4 buckets of cement. How many buckets of sand do I need?

> A **ratio** is a way of comparing two or more quantities.

cement : sand

> Find the multiplier.
> Multiply each part.

I need ..... buckets.

2 Tick the ratios which are equivalent to the ratio 1 : 4.

   a 2 : 2   **b** 3 : 12

   c 10 : 40   **d** 8 : 2

> The ratios 2 : 5 and 4 : 10 are called **equivalent ratios**.
> Equivalent ratios show the same proportion.
> Both sides of a ratio are multiplied or divided by the same number to give an equivalent ratio.

3 STEM 50 ml of vinegar reacts with 25 ml of calcium carbonate solution.

   a Write the ratio of vinegar to calcium carbonate solution. ....

   b How much calcium carbonate solution is needed to react with 200 ml of vinegar? ....

   c How much vinegar is needed to react with 75 ml of calcium carbonate solution? ....

4 Write each ratio in its simplest form.

   a 4 : 8 ....   **b** 20 : 2 ....   **c** 15 : 35 ....

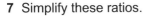

> You can make the numbers in a ratio as small as possible by **simplifying**. You simplify a ratio by dividing the numbers in the ratio by the **highest common factor.**

5 Real Sandra puts 1000 ml of petrol and 20 ml of oil into her chainsaw.
The recommended ratio of petrol to oil is 50 : 1.

   Is Sandra's ratio of petrol to oil correct? ....

6 Write each ratio in its simplest form.

   a 2 : 4 : 8 ....

   b 10 : 20 : 15 ....

   c 8 : 16 : 100 ....

> The highest common factor of 2, 4 and 8 is ☐.

7 Simplify these ratios.

   a £5 : 70p   **b** 2 days : 10 hours   **c** 3 km : 120 m

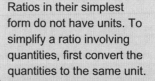

> Ratios in their simplest form do not have units. To simplify a ratio involving quantities, first convert the quantities to the same unit.

8 Write these ratios in their simplest form.

   a 3 : 3.5 ....

   b $1 : 1\frac{1}{3}$ ....

   c $4 : 1\frac{1}{5}$ ....

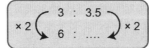

> For a ratio with fractions or decimals, first multiply both sides of the ratio to get whole numbers.

CHECK Tick each box as your **confidence** in this topic improves.

Need extra help? Go to page 80 and tick the boxes next to Q2, 3 and 4. Then have a go at it once you've finished 8.1–8.6.

1 Share these amounts in the ratios given. Show how you check your answers.

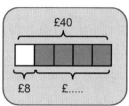

a £40 in the ratio 1 : 4

1 + 4 = 5 parts

5 parts = £40

1 part = £40 ÷ 5 = £8

4 parts = £8 × 4 = £........

£8 : £........

Check: 8 + ... = 40 ——— Check your answer by adding the parts.

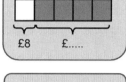
£8   £.....

b £21 in the ratio 3 : 4

2 Problem-solving Mrs Jones has a body fat to body mass ratio of 1 : 3.
Mrs Jones has a body mass of 60 kg.
Mr Jones has a body fat to body mass ratio of 1 : 4.
Mr Jones has a body mass of 80 kg.
Who has the greater mass of body fat?

3 Share these amounts in the ratios given. Show how you check your answers.

a £60 in the ratio 1 : 2 : 3

1 + 2 + 3 = 6 parts

6 parts = £60 ———

1 part = £60 ÷ ...... = £ ......

2 parts = £...... × 2 = £ ......

3 parts = £...... × 3 = £ ......

£ ...... : £...... : £......

Check: ...... + ... + ... = 60

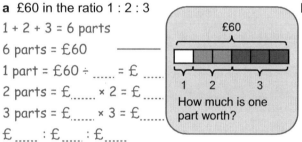
£60

1   2   3

How much is one part worth?

b £549 in the ratio 2 : 4 : 3

Worked example

4 STEM An alloy is made from copper, manganese and zinc in the ratio 14 : 3 : 3.
140 g of alloy is made. How much copper is used?

5 Problem-solving A jeweller makes the alloy called pink gold by mixing
gold, copper and silver in the ratio 15 : 4 : 1.

a The jeweller has 32 g of copper. How many grams are needed of

i gold ....

ii silver? ....

b How many grams of pink gold does the jeweller mix altogether?

6 Problem-solving The sides of a quadrilateral are in the ratio 2 : 4 : 5 : 9.
The shortest side is 6 cm. Calculate the perimeter of the quadrilateral.

The shortest side is 6 cm.
How many parts is this?

CHECK Tick each box as your **confidence** in this topic improves.

Need extra help? Go to page 80 and tick the boxes next to Q5, 6 and 7. Then have a go at them once you've finished 8.1–8.6.

1 Gerry has collected 10 autographs. 6 of them are from footballers, the rest are from rugby players.

Guided

a Write the ratio of footballers to rugby players in its simplest form.

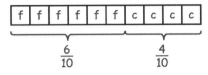

football : rugby

$\div 2 \left(\begin{array}{ccc} 6 & : & 4 \\ 3 & : & .... \end{array} \right) \div 2$

> Ratio compares part to part.
> Proportion compares part to whole.
> Proportions can be written
> as fractions or percentages.

b What proportion of the autographs are from footballers?

| f | f | f | f | f | f | c | c | c | c |

$\frac{6}{10}$ $\frac{4}{10}$

Write your answer as **i** a fraction .... **ii** a percentage. ....

2 Real In the 2006 Commonwealth Games, India won gold, silver and bronze medals
in the ratio 22 : 17 : 11.

a What proportion of the medals were gold? ....

b What proportion of the medals were bronze? ....

Write your answers as a fraction and as a percentage.

 3 Real / Problem-solving Retired basketball player Michael Jordan scored 32 292 points in 1073
professional games. Kareem Abdul-Jabbar scored 38 387 points in 1560 professional games.
Who has the better points to games ratio?

4 Problem-solving John and Gill make green paint.
The ratio of blue to yellow in John's green is 3 : 4.
The ratio of blue to yellow in Gill's green is 2 : 3.
Use proportions to explain whose green has more yellow in it.

> Write the proportions
> as fractions.

5 Real Akiva divides his earnings like this:

65% for rent/household bills, 25% for food/car/fun, 10% for savings.

Write the ratio of rent/household to food/car/fun to savings, in its simplest form.

6 Real Approximately $\frac{3}{5}$ of an adult male's body mass is water and $\frac{2}{5}$ is other chemicals.
Write this as a ratio.

CHECK Tick each box as your
confidence in this
topic improves.

Need extra help? Go to page 81 and tick the
boxes next to Q8 and 9. Then have a go at
them once you've finished 8.1–8.6.

Guided

1 Yanto uses 120 g of raisins to make 6 scones.
What quantity of raisins would he need to make 9 scones?

6 scones + 3 scones = 9 scones

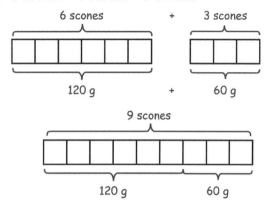

> When two quantities are in **direct proportion,** as one increases or decreases, the other increases or decreases in the same ratio.

120 g + ... g = ... g

2 Two kilograms of bananas cost £1.20. Work out the cost of

a 4 kg .... **b** 6 kg .... **c** 1 kg .... **d** 5 kg. ....

3 Problem-solving To make 100 kg of waterproof concrete, Juan mixes 1 bag of cement, 10 buckets of sand and 2 litres of waterproofer.
Juan needs 350 kg of waterproof concrete. He has 4 bags of cement, 30 buckets of sand and 11 litres of waterproofer. Does he have enough of the materials?

> Show your working. Write a sentence to answer the question.

4 Real / Problem-solving 4 women dig a vegetable plot in 6 hours.

Guided

a How long would it take 8 women to dig it?

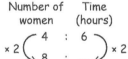

Number of women   Time (hours)

$\times 2 \begin{pmatrix} 4 & : & 6 \\ 8 & : & .... \end{pmatrix} \times 2$

> When two quantities are in **inverse proportion**, as one increases, the other decreases in the same ratio.

b How long would it take 1 woman to dig it?

> The fewer people there are, the more time it takes. Dividing the number of people by 4 means you have to multiply the time by ☐.

5 Problem-solving It takes 100 minutes to drive home at 30 mph.

a How long will it take to drive home at a speed of

   i 60 mph   **ii** 15 mph   **iii** 50 mph?

b What speed is needed to drive home in 1 hour?

CHECK Tick each box as your **confidence** in this topic improves.

Need extra help? Go to page 81 and tick the boxes next to Q10, 13 and 14. Then have a go at them once you've finished 8.1–8.6.

8.6 Using the unitary method

1 3 pineapples cost £3.60.

   a Work out the cost of

      i 1 pineapple   **ii** 4 pineapples.

> Using the unitary method means finding the value of 1 part.

```
        pineapples  cost
     ÷3 ⌒  3    : £3.60  ⌐ ÷3
        ⌊  1    : £.........  ⌡
```

   b How many pineapples can you buy for £7.20? ....

2 5 ice creams cost £6.50.
How much do 11 ice creams cost?

> Work out the cost of 1 ice cream first.

3 **Problem-solving**   Tim earns £42 for 7 hours' work.

   a Tim works for 16 hours. How much does he earn?

> Find how much he gets paid for 1 hour first.

   b Tim earns 'time and a half' for overtime. He works 4 hours of overtime in addition to his normal 16 hours. How much does he earn altogether?

> 'Time and a half' means one and a half times as much as normal pay.

4 **Finance / Real / Problem-solving**   A supermarket sells kiwi fruit at £1.50 for a 6-pack and £2.25 for a 10-pack.
Which pack is better value for money?

> Work out how much it costs to buy 1 kiwi fruit first and then compare.

5 Write these ratios in the form $1 : n$.

   a 3 : 12   **b** 2 : 20   **c** 0.5 : 0.2   **d** 500 cm : 2 m

```
     ÷3 ⌒  3   :  12   ⌐ ÷3
        ⌊  1   :  ......... ⌡
```

6 Write 3 m to 20 mm as a ratio in the form $n : 1$. ....

7 **Problem-solving**   Olaf made hot chocolate using chocolate powder and hot water in the ratio 10 : 250. Helga made another drink using chocolate powder and hot water in the ratio 15 : 360.

   a Write each of these ratios in the form $1 : n$.

   b Whose drink was stronger?

> **Worked example**
>
>

CHECK   Tick each box as your **confidence** in this topic improves.

Need extra help? Go to page 81 and tick the boxes next to Q10, 11 and 12. Then have a go at them once you've finished 8.1–8.6.

8 Strengthen

Ratio and measures

miles 0 1 2
× 1.6
km 0 1.6 ☐
÷ 1.6

 ☐ **1** Complete these.

   a 5 miles ≈ .... km   **b** $\frac{1}{4}$ mile ≈ .... km

   c 6 gallons ≈ .... litres   **d** 4 feet ≈ .... cm

   e 20 lb ≈ .... kg

☐ **2** Write each ratio in its simplest form.

   a 3 : 15

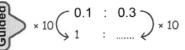

Guided

÷ 3 ⟨ 3 : 15 ⟩ ÷ 3
.... : ....

> 3 is the largest number you can divide both 3 and 15 by.

   b 2 : 22

Worked example

☐ **3** Write each ratio in its simplest form.

   a 0.1 : 0.3   **b** 0.2 : 0.6   **c** 0.4 : 0.8

> Multiply by 10 to get whole numbers, then simplify if needed.

Guided

× 10 ⟨ 0.1 : 0.3 ⟩ × 10
     1 : ....

   d $\frac{1}{5} : \frac{4}{5}$ **e** $\frac{2}{7} : \frac{3}{7}$ **f** $\frac{2}{8} : \frac{6}{8}$

× 5 ⟨ $\frac{1}{5}$: $\frac{4}{5}$ ⟩ × 5
    .... : ....

> Multiply by the denominator to get whole numbers, then simplify if needed.

☐ **4** Write each ratio in its simplest form.

   a 20p : £3.00   **b** £3.20 : 40p   **c** 600 g : 2 kg

> Write both parts in the same units first.
> 20p : 300p
> ☐ : ☐

☐ **5** Share these amounts in the ratio given.

   a £40 in the ratio 1 : 3   **b** £35 in the ratio 4 : 1   **c** £56 in the ratio 3 : 4

Guided

£40

£..... £.....

☐ **6** Share these amounts in the ratios given.

   a £21 in the ratio 1 : 2 : 4   **b** £200 in the ratio 1 : 4 : 5

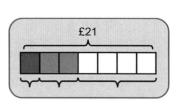

£21

☐ **7** **Problem-solving** The angles of a triangle are in the ratio 1 : 3 : 5.
Calculate the size of each angle.

> The angles of a triangle sum to 180°.

Direct and inverse proportion

Guided **8** There are 4 boys and 6 girls on a school minibus.

    a How many students are on the minibus? 4 + 6 = 10

    b What proportion of the students are boys? $\frac{....}{10}$

    c Write the fraction in part **b** in its simplest form. ....

    d What proportion of the students are girls?

       Write your answer as a percentage. ....

students

boys   girls

9 **Reasoning** In a surfing competition, Jo has a ratio of perfect-score runs to wipeouts of 1 : 9.

    a What percentage of Jo's runs are perfect? ....

   Ben has a perfect-score run to wipeout ratio of 3 : 2.

    b What percentage of Ben's runs are perfect? ....

    c Who would probably win in a surfing competition

       between Ben and Jo? ....

100%

| P | W | W | W | W | W | W | W | W | W |

...... %   ...... %

10 4 pizzas cost £20. Work out the cost of

    a 1 pizza ....

    b 5 pizzas ....

    c 11 pizzas. ....

4 pizzas

£20

Worked example

11 In shop A, 20 pens cost £4.80. In shop B, 30 pens cost £7.50.

    a How much does one pen cost in shop A? ....

    b How much does one pen cost in shop B? ....

    c Which shop offers better value for money? ....

12 Katy has two cars.
The red car travels 40 km on 4 litres of fuel.
The blue car travels 60 km on 5 litres of fuel.

    a For each car, write a ratio to show the number of km to litres. ....

    b Express each ratio in the form n : 1. ....

    c Which car is more economical to run? ....

Literacy hint
'Economical'
means cheaper.

Guided **13** It takes one student 12 hours to build a go-cart. How long will it take

    a 2 students   **b** 3 students?

   students hours

    ×2 (1 : 12) ÷2

          2 : ....

Multiply and divide by the same number.

14 It takes 10 students 4 hours to build a tree platform. How long does it take

    a 5 students   **b** 20 students   **c** 1 student?

1 **Problem-solving** Allen is 10 years old. Haley is 2 years older than Allen and 4 years younger than Tony. Write the ratio of Allen's age to Haley's age to Tony's age in its simplest form.

Guided

2 Convert these amounts into the units shown.

a $3 \text{ lb} \approx 3 \div 2.2 \approx 1.36 \text{ kg}$ = ... g

b $6 \text{ ft} \approx 6 \times 30 \approx$ .... cm = ... m

c 4 miles ≈ .... km = ... m

d 9 gallons ≈ .... litres = ... m*l*

e 5 pints ≈ .... litres = ... m*l*

f 30 inches ≈ .... cm ≈ .... m

3 **Problem-solving** In a class there are 10 boys. There are 5 more girls than boys.
What proportion of the class are girls? Write your answer as a fraction and as a percentage.

4 The table shows the numbers of matches two hockey teams win, lose and draw in a season.

Team	Win	Lose	Draw
A	5	3	2
B	6	3	0

a Write the proportion of matches lost by each team as a percentage. ....

b Which team loses the higher proportion of matches? ....

5 **STEM / Problem-solving** 2 kg of bronze is made from approximately 1.8 kg of copper and 200 g of tin.

a Write this ratio in its simplest form. ....

b A small bronze statue contains 100 g of copper.
How much does the statue weigh?

6 Three divers did a sponsored river clean-up to raise money for charity.
Neal picked up twice as much litter as Dave. Dave picked up 3 times as much as Zander.

a Write the ratio of litter picked up by Neal, Dave and Zander. ....

b Altogether they picked up 80 kg of litter. How much did each person pick up?

7 **Problem-solving** A chef chops onions, potatoes and carrots in the ratio 7 : 1 : 2.
She chops 40 onions and potatoes altogether.
How many carrots does she chop?

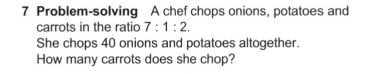

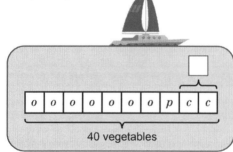

| o | o | o | o | o | o | o | p | c | c |

40 vegetables

8 **Problem-solving / Reasoning**   A can holds 330 ml of drink.
A supermarket has two deals:

6 × 330 ml cans for £2.90 and 10 × 330 ml cans for £4.75.

a Work out how much 1 can costs in each deal.

£2.90 ÷ 6 = 290p ÷ 6 = ... each   £4.75 ÷ 10 = ... each

b Which deal is the better value for money? ....

9 **Finance / Problem-solving**   Each week Fran spends $\frac{1}{2}$ of her pocket money on music downloads
and $\frac{1}{6}$ on judo lessons. She saves the rest.

Write the ratio of her spending on music downloads to judo to saving, in its simplest form.

> Work out the fraction of her pocket money she saves.

10 **Problem-solving**   In a health food shop, $\frac{1}{4}$ of the chocolate bars are dairy-free.

Write the ratio of chocolate bars with dairy to dairy-free chocolate bars in its simplest form.

> Work out the fraction of bars that are not dairy-free first.

11 **Problem-solving**   Each month Dom spends 15% of his paper round wages on music downloads
and 25% on judo lessons. He saves the rest.

a Write the ratio of his spending on music downloads to judo to saving,
in its simplest form.

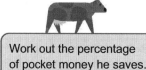

> Work out the percentage of pocket money he saves.

b One week he spends £9 on music downloads and £15 on judo.
How much does he save?

12 **STEM**   The table gives the power (in horse power) and mass (in tonnes) of three cars.

Car	Mass, m (t)	Power, p (hp)	Mass : power (1 : n)
A	1.1	880	
B	1.25	155	
C	1.32	118	

Write the ratio of mass to power for each car in the form 1 : n.

13 **Problem-solving**   It takes 16 artists 30 hours to paint a mural.

a How long would it take 4 artists? ....

b How many artists are needed to paint the mural in 40 hours? ....

PROGRESS BAR Colour in the progress bar as you get questions correct.
Then fill in the progression chart on pages 107–109.

1 Write the ratio 12 : 16 in its simplest form. ....

2 Share £30 in the ratio 2 : 3. ....

3 Write each ratio in its simplest form.

a 15 : 20 : 30 ....   b 1 day : 10 hours ....   c £4.50 : 90p ....

4 Complete these.

a 8 lb ≈ .... g   b 20 miles ≈ .... km   c 2 ft ≈ .... cm

5 In a garden the ratio of vegetables to flowers is 1 : 4. Write this ratio as

a a fraction ....   b a percentage. ....

6 4 sandwiches cost £10. Work out the cost of 3 sandwiches.

7 Share £320 in the ratio 1 : 2 : 5.

8 A shop sells doughnuts.
The shop has 3 different deals on doughnuts.

Which offer is the best value for money?

Offer 1

2 doughnuts

90p

Offer 2

5 doughnuts

£2

Offer 3

12 doughnuts

£5.40

9 Write the ratio 0.6 : 0.9 in its simplest form. ....

10 Write these ratios in the form 1 : n.

a 5 : 25 ....   b 0.3 : 1.2 ....

11 Write these ratios in the form n : 1.

a 18 : 2 ....   b 5 : 25 ....

12 It takes 4 students 8 hours to build a robot.

a How long does it take

i 2 students ....   ii 8 students? ....

b How many students are needed to build the robot in 1 hour? ....

9.1 Triangles, parallelograms and trapeziums

1 Work out the area of each parallelogram.

a
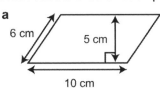
6 cm · 5 cm · 10 cm

b
2 m · 6.5 m · 1 m

Area of a parallelogram
= base length ×
    perpendicular height
= $b \times h$
= bh
The perpendicular height is
the height measured at right
angles to the base.

Area of a parallelogram = bh

= 10 × 5 = ...

2 Work out the missing measurement for this parallelogram.

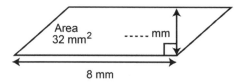
Area 32 mm² ····· mm · 8 mm

3 Work out the area of each triangle.

a
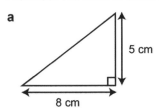
5 cm · 8 cm

b
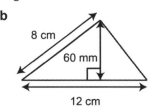
8 cm · 60 mm · 12 cm

c
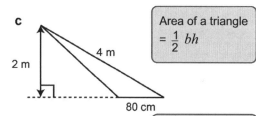
4 m · 2 m · 80 cm

Area of a triangle
= $\frac{1}{2} bh$

Area = $\frac{1}{2} bh$

= $\frac{1}{2}$ × .... × .... = ...

Make sure all the
lengths for each
shape are in the
same units.

4 Work out the missing measurement
for this triangle.

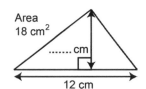
Area 18 cm² · .... cm · 12 cm

Substitute the values you
know into the formula for
area, then solve the equation.

5 Problem-solving Steve makes a flag from black and grey cloth. The three triangles are isosceles.
Work out the total area of cloth Steve needs.

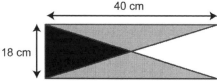
40 cm · 18 cm

6 Work out the area of each trapezium.

a
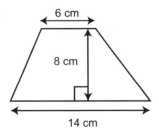
6 cm · 8 cm · 14 cm

b
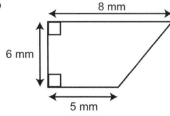
8 mm · 6 mm · 5 mm

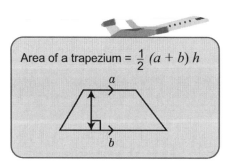
Area of a trapezium = $\frac{1}{2}(a + b)h$

a · b

CHECK · Tick each box as your **confidence** in this topic improves.

Need extra help? Go to page 91 and tick the boxes next to Q1, 2, 4 and 5. Then have a go at them once you've finished 9.1–9.6.

85

9.2 Perimeter and area of compound shapes

1 Work out each missing side length.

a

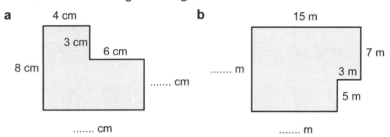

4 cm
3 cm
6 cm
8 cm
.... cm
.... cm

b

15 m
7 m
3 m
.... m
5 m
.... m

4 cm
6 cm

☐ ☐
☐ cm

Work out the two missing lengths. Write them on the diagram.

2 Work out the perimeter of this shape.

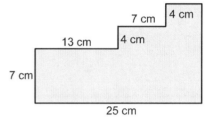

7 cm   4 cm
13 cm   4 cm
7 cm
25 cm

3 Real The diagrams show the dimensions of two rooms.
Work out the area of carpet needed for each room.

a

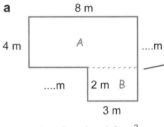

8 m
4 m   A   ....m
....m   2 m B
3 m

Divide the shape into 2 rectangles, A and B. Work out any missing lengths.

Area A = 8 × 4 = 32 m²
Area B = ... × ..... = ... m²
Total = 32 + ... = ... m²

Work out the area of A and the area of B and then add them together.

b

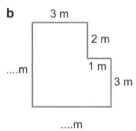

3 m
2 m
....m   1 m
3 m
....m

Worked example

[QR code]

4 Problem-solving Work out the shaded area of each shape.

a

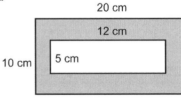

20 cm
12 cm
10 cm   5 cm

b

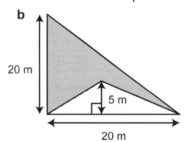

20 m
20 m
5 m
20 m

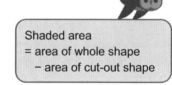

Shaded area
= area of whole shape
  − area of cut-out shape

5 Real / Problem-solving Three congruent trapeziums and two congruent parallelograms are pressed out of a metal strip. What area of the metal strip is unused?

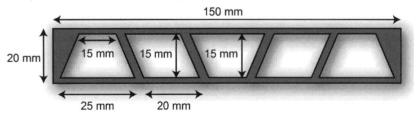

150 mm
20 mm
15 mm 15 mm 15 mm
25 mm   20 mm

CHECK   Tick each box as your **confidence** in this topic improves.
☹ ☺ ☺
☐ ☐ ☐

Need extra help? Go to page 91 and tick the box next to Q3. Then have a go at it once you've finished 9.1–9.6.

86

1 Sketch a net for each cuboid.

a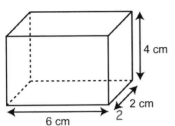

4 cm

6 cm

2 cm

b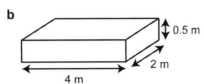

0.5 m

4 m

2 m

A **net** is a 2D shape that folds to make a 3D solid.

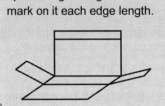

Imagine breaking the cuboid apart along its edges. Then mark on it each edge length.

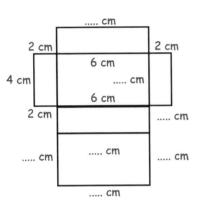

..... cm

2 cm   2 cm

6 cm

4 cm   ..... cm

6 cm

2 cm

..... cm   ..... cm

..... cm   ..... cm   ..... cm

..... cm

For a sketch you should use a ruler and a pencil, but you don't need to measure the lengths accurately.

2 Look at these nets.

A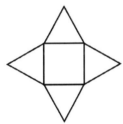

B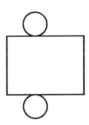

C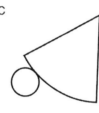

Which one folds to make **a** a cone ...... **b** a square-based pyramid ...... **c** a cylinder? ......

3 Write down the number of faces, edges and vertices in this cuboid.

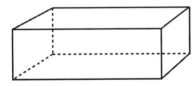

faces ....

edges ....

vertices ....

3D shapes have faces (flat surfaces), edges (where two faces meet) and vertices (corners). One corner is called a vertex.

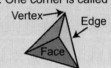

Vertex   Edge

Face

4 Problem-solving Look at this cuboid.
You can cut a cuboid into two equal parts.
Sketch the new 3D shapes you would make if you cut it

a horizontally   **b** vertically   **c** diagonally.

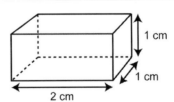

1 cm

1 cm

2 cm

CHECK   Tick each box as your **confidence** in this topic improves.

Need extra help? Go to page 92 and tick the box next to Q8. Then have a go at it once you've finished 9.1–9.6.

9.4 Surface area

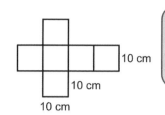

1 The diagrams show a cube and its net.
Work out the surface area of the cube.

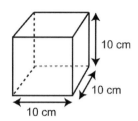

10 cm
10 cm
10 cm
10 cm
10 cm
10 cm

> The surface area of a 3D shape is the total area of all its faces.

2 What is the surface area of each cube?

a

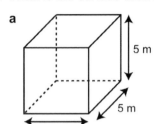

5 m
5 m
5 m

b a 2 mm by 2 mm by 2 mm cube

c a cube with edge length 1 cm

3 Work out the surface area of each cuboid.

a

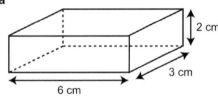

2 cm
3 cm
6 cm

b

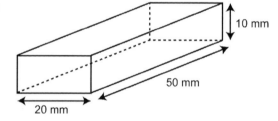

10 mm
50 mm
20 mm

Guided

Surface area
Area of top face = 6 × 3 = 18 cm²
Area of front face = 6 × ...... = ... cm²
Area of side face = ... × ...... = ... cm²
Sum of 3 faces = ... + ... + ... = ... cm²
Total surface area = 2 × ...... = ... cm²

4 Problem-solving A cube has a surface area of 96 cm².

a What is the area of each face? _____

b What is the length of one edge? _____

5 Real / Problem-solving Farouq wants to paint the outside of this metal container.
He cannot paint underneath the container.
He has 4 cans of paint. Each can covers 20 m².
Will this be enough?

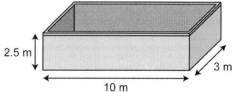

2.5 m
10 m
3 m

Worked example

CHECK Tick each box as your **confidence** in this topic improves.

Need extra help? Go to page 92 and tick the box next to Q7. Then have a go at it once you've finished 9.1–9.6.

9.5 Volume

1 A cube has a side length of 5 cm. What is the volume of the cube?

Volume of a cube = side length (*l*) cubed = *l*³ = 5³ = ... cm³

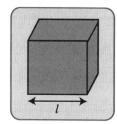

2 Problem-solving A cube has a surface area of 96 cm².

   a What is the area of one face? ....

   b What is the length of one side? ....

   c What is the volume of the cube? ....

> **Strategy hint**
> Sketch a cube.

> The **volume** of a solid shape is the amount of 3D space it takes up. The units of volume are cubic units (e.g. mm³, cm³, m³).

3 Calculate the volume of each cuboid.

   a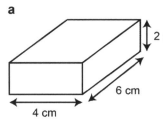

   b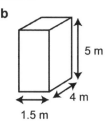

   c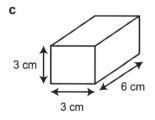

> Volume of a cuboid
> = length × width × height
> = *l* × *w* × *h*
> = *lwh*
>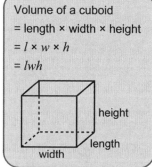

Volume = *lwh*

= 6 × 4 × 2

= .... cm³

4 Complete these conversions.

   a 0.25 litres = ... cm³

   b 5 cm³ = ... m*l*

   c .... litres = 5125 cm³

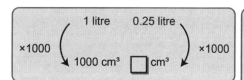

> The capacity of a container is how much it can hold. The units of capacity are cm³, millilitres (m*l*) and litres (*l*).
> • 1 millilitre (m*l*) = 1 cm³
> • 1 litre (*l*) = 1000 cm³

5 Real / Reasoning For a drive through Spain in the summer, Greg buys a car-fridge with internal measurements 25 cm by 20 cm by 30 cm.

   a Work out the capacity in cm³. ....

   b Work out the capacity in litres. ....

Greg estimates that he will be able to fit seven 2-litre bottles of water in the fridge.

   c Explain why he might be wrong.

6 Problem-solving A 10 cm by 10 cm by 10 cm cube has a 5 cm by 5 cm square hole cut through it. What is the volume of the remaining solid?

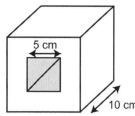

> What is the volume of the piece cut out of the cube?

> CHECK   Tick each box as your **confidence** in this topic improves.
>

> **Need extra help?** Go to page 92 and tick the box next to Q8. Then have a go at it once you've finished 9.1–9.6.

1 Which unit of area would be sensible for measuring

   a the area of a smartphone ....

   b the area of Italy ....

   c the area of a netball court? ....

> It is important to be able to choose the most suitable metric units for measuring. Some of the metric units that you already know are
> - mm, cm, m, km (length)
> - mm^2, cm^2, m^2, km^2, hectares (area)

2 Real A rectangular runway measures 2.4 km by 250 m. How many hectares is this?

Guided

Area = 2.4 km × 250 m = 2400 × 250 = ... m^2

Number of hectares = ... ÷ .... = ...

> Convert km to m and then m^2 to hectares. A hectare is 10 000 m^2.

3 These squares are the same size.

   a Write in the missing measurements.

   b Work out the area of

      i square A .... cm^2 **ii** square B .... mm^2

   c Complete these sentences.

      i To convert from cm^2 to mm^2 .... by ....

      ii To convert from mm^2 to cm^2 .... by ....

1 cm | A
1 cm

...... mm | B
...... mm

4 Complete these conversions.

Guided

   a 8 cm^2 = 8 × 10^2 = 800 mm^2

   b 57 500 cm^2 = ... m^2

   c .... cm^2 = 950 mm^2

   d .... m^2 = 8.5 km^2

   e 0.2 m^2 = ... cm^2

   f 4500 m^2 = ... km^2

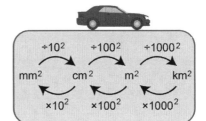

$÷10^2$ $÷100^2$ $÷1000^2$

mm^2 cm^2 m^2 km^2

$×10^2$ $×100^2$ $×1000^2$

> **Worked example**

5 Problem-solving The base of a swimming pool is to be tiled using small square tiles of side length 2 cm.
The base is a 12 m by 4 m rectangle. How many tiles are needed?

6 Complete these conversions.

   a 12 cm^3 = ... mm^3 **b** .... cm^3 = 66 mm^3

   c 1.75 m^3 = ... cm^3 **d** .... m^3 = 125 000 cm^3

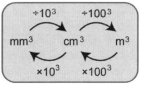

$÷10^3$ $÷100^3$

mm^3 cm^3 m^3

$×10^3$ $×100^3$

7 Problem-solving A toy manufacturer needs to ship 100 000 toys from China to the USA. Each toy is in a box measuring 25 cm × 25 cm × 10 cm, and the shipping containers measure 12 m × 2.5 m × 2.5 m. How many containers does the company need to transport all 100 000 toys at once?

> CHECK   Tick each box as your **confidence** in this topic improves.

> **Need extra help?** Go to page 92 and tick the boxes next to Q9, 10 and 11. Then have a go at them once you've finished 9.1–9.6.

9 Strengthen

Area and perimeter of 2D shapes

1 Find the area of the rectangle and the area of the triangle.

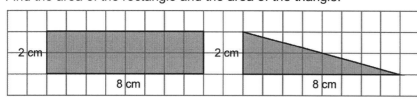

> Area of a triangle
> $= \frac{1}{2} \times$ base length
> $\times$ perpendicular height

area of rectangle = ...

area of triangle = ...

2 a For this triangle, write down

    i the base length .... cm

    ii the perpendicular height .... cm

  b Work out the area of the triangle. ....

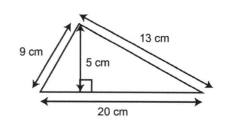

3 For this shape work out

  a the perimeter   **b** the area.

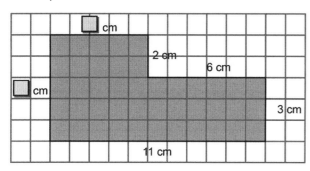

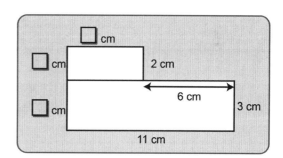

  a Perimeter = 11 + 3 + 6 + 2 + ... + ... = ... cm

  b Area = ... × .... + ... × .... = ... + ... = ... cm²

4 Calculate the area of the parallelogram.

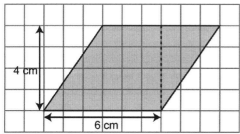

> Imagine making the parallelogram into a rectangle by moving part of the shape to the other side.
>
>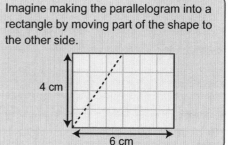

5 Calculate the area of the trapezium.

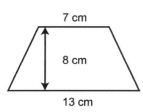

Area = $\frac{1}{2}(a + b)h$

$= \frac{1}{2} \times ($ .... + ... $) \times$ ....

$= \frac{1}{2} \times$ .... $\times$ ....

$=$ .... cm²

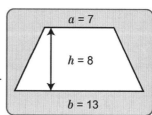

Worked example

Working with 3D solids

Guided

☐ **6** Write down the number of faces, edges and vertices in this cube.

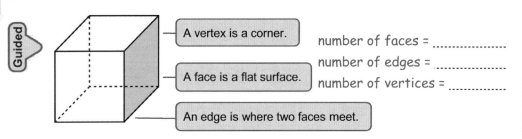

A vertex is a corner.

A face is a flat surface.

An edge is where two faces meet.

number of faces = ...

number of edges = ...

number of vertices = ...

A vertex is one corner, vertices are more than one corner.

Guided

☐ **7** Complete the table to find the surface area of the cuboid.

Face	Area
Top	$5 \times 2 = 10$ cm^2
Bottom	
Front	$5 \times 3 = 15$ cm^2
Back	
Left	$2 \times 3 = 6$ cm^2
Right	
Total surface area	

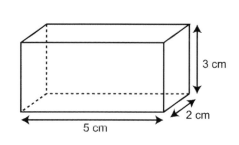

☐ **8** Calculate the volume of each cuboid.

a

10 cm

2 cm

4 cm

b

1 cm

10 cm

5 cm

c

2 cm

2 cm

2 cm

Guided

Volume = $l \times w \times h$

= 10 × 4 × 2

= .... cm^3

Measures of area and volume

Guided

☐ **9 a** Work out the area of the rectangle in cm^2.

Area = ... × .... = ...

b Convert the area of the rectangle to mm^2. ....

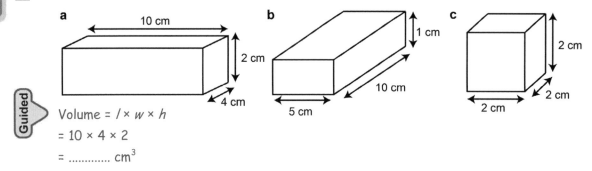

8 cm

2 cm

cm^2 1   2   3

×100   ÷100

mm^2 100   200   300

Guided

☐ **10 a** Work out the area of the rectangle in m^2.

Area = ... × .... = ...

b Convert the area of the rectangle to cm^2. ....

3 m

12 m

cm^2 1   2   3

×10 000   ÷10 000

mm^2 10 000   20 000   30 000

☐ **11** Complete these conversions.

a i 8 cm^3 = ... mm^3 **ii** .... cm^3 = 22 500 mm^3

b i 0.03 m^3 = ... cm^3 **ii** .... m^3 = 6.5 million cm^3

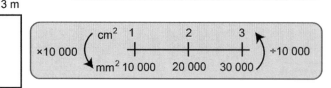

cm^3 1   2   3   5

×☐   ÷☐

mm^3 1000   3000   4000   5000

1 Reasoning

a Find the area of this shape by adding together the areas of A and B.

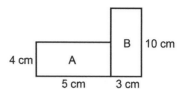

b Find the area of the same shape again. This time, find the area of the whole rectangle and subtract the shaded area.

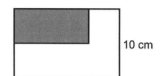

2 The area of this L shape is 52 cm². Find the perimeter of the shape.

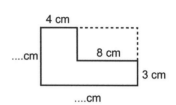

3 The volume of water in a swimming pool in the shape of a cuboid is 120 m³. The pool is 15 m long and 5 m wide. The water comes to 12 cm from the top of the pool.

a Calculate the depth of water in the pool.

Volume = base × height × width

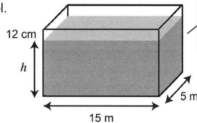

Sketch the water in the pool. Put the measurements you know on your sketch.

Worked example

b How much more water is required to fill the pool to 2 cm from the top?

4 Deep Sea World has an orca tank with a capacity of 4500 cubic metres.

a Write possible dimensions for the tank in

i metres x = ... m, y = ... m, z = ... m

ii feet x = ... ft, y = ... ft, z = ... ft

b Calculate the volume of the tank in cubic feet.

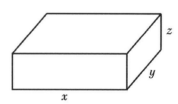

1 m ≈ 3 ft

5 Work out the shaded area of each shape.

a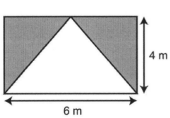

b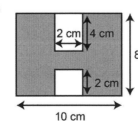

c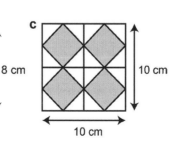

6 Reasoning Look at this cuboid.

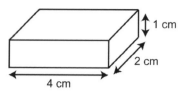

a Calculate the volume of the cuboid. ....

b Calculate the surface area of the cuboid. ....

c How can four of these cuboids be put together to make a cuboid with the smallest surface area?

7 Calculate the volume of each solid.

a

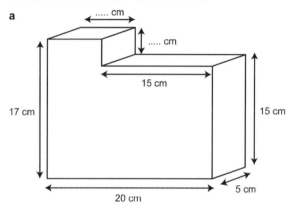

b

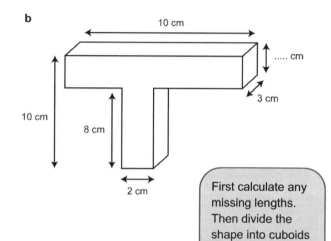

First calculate any missing lengths. Then divide the shape into cuboids and work out the volume of each cuboid separately.

8 Each of these shapes has an area of 24 cm². Find the missing numbers.

a

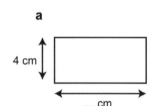

b

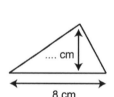

c

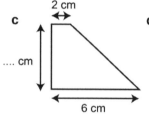

d

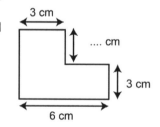

9 Calculate the surface area of this triangular prism.

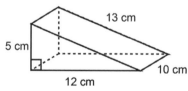

A triangular prism has .... faces.

There are .... triangles and .... rectangles.

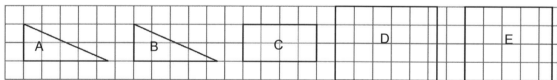

Area of triangle A = $\frac{1}{2}$ × .... × .... = ... cm²

Area of triangle B = $\frac{1}{2}$ × .... × .... = ... cm²

Area of rectangle C = ... × .... = ... cm²

Area of rectangle D = ...

Area of rectangle E = ...

Surface area = ...

9 Unit test

1 For this shape work out

   a the perimeter ....

   b the area. ....

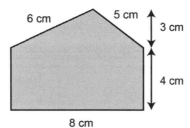

2 For each shape work out   **i** the volume   **ii** the surface area.

  a

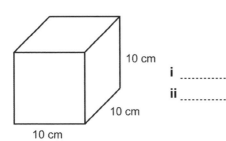

   i ....

   ii ....

  b

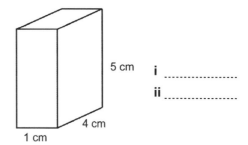

   i ....

   ii ....

3 Work out the area of each shape.

  a

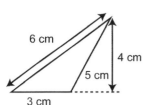

  b

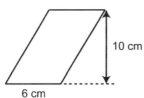

  c

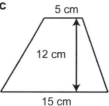

4 The square and the rectangle have the same area. Work out

   a the area of the square in m^2 ....

   b the area of the square in cm^2 ....

   c the area of the square in mm^2 ....

   d the missing length in cm. ....

5 Work out the volume of this solid.

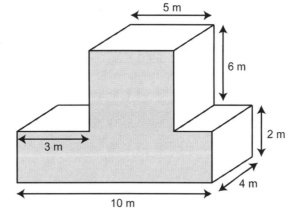

6 Complete these conversions.

   a $7.2\ m^3 =$ .... cm^3 **b** .... $cm^3 = 9900\ mm^3$ **c** $630\ ml =$ .... cm^3

1 Here is a sequence of positive odd numbers.

1, 3, 5, 7, ..., 11, 13, 15, ...

a Write in the missing term.

b Is the sequence ascending or descending? ....

c Is the sequence finite or infinite? ....

> Numbers in a **sequence** are called **terms**.
> Numbers *increase* in **ascending** sequences.
> Numbers *decrease* in **descending** sequences.
> A **finite** sequence has a fixed number of terms.
> An **infinite** sequence goes on forever.

2 Describe each sequence by giving the 1st term and the term-to-term rule.

a 4, 6, 8, 10, ... 1st term = ..., rule: add 2

b 3, 8, 13, 18, ... 1st term = 3, rule: ....

c 20, 17, 14, 11, ...

d 12, 12.5, 13, 13.5, ...

> **Worked example**
>
>

> You can describe a sequence by giving the 1st term and the **term-to-term rule**.
> The term-to-term rule tells you how to get from one term to the next.

3 Tick the arithmetic sequences.

a 77, 76, 75, 74, ...   **b** 2, 4, 8, 16, ...

c 5, 6, 5, 6, 5, ...   **d** 3, 6, 9, 12, ...

> An **arithmetic** sequence goes up or down in equal steps. This step is called the **common difference**.

4 Work out the first five terms of each arithmetic sequence.

a 1st term = 3   common difference = 2   3, 5, 7, ...

b 1st term = 0   common difference = 10   ....

c 1st term = 20   common difference = –10   ....

d 1st term = 8   common difference = –3   ....

5 Describe each arithmetic sequence by writing the 1st term and the common difference.

a 100, 105, 110, 115, ...

b 7, 10, 13, 16, ...

c 50, 30, 10, –10, ...

d 20, 11, 2, –7, ...

6 Sally decides to increase the number of sit-ups she does by 2 each day.

a Continue the sequence to show how many sit-ups she does for the first week.

1, 3, 5, ...

b On which day will Sally first do more than 30 sit-ups? ....

7 The first five terms of a sequence are 4, 8, 12, 16, 20.

a What is the 10th term? ....

b What is the 50th term? ....

c What is the 100th term? ....

> n is the term number.
> **1st 2nd 3rd 4th** ...
> n is always a positive integer.
> You can describe a sequence by giving the **general term** (or nth term). The general term relates the term number, n, to the term.

CHECK Tick each box as your **confidence** in this topic improves.

Need extra help? Go to page 101 and tick the boxes next to Q1, 2, 4 and 5. Then have a go at them once you've finished 10.1–10.5.

10.2 The nth term

1 The general term of a sequence is $4n$

  a Write the first five terms in the sequence.

  1st term, 2nd term, 3rd term, 4th term, 5th term

    4×1 4×2 4×3 4×4 4×5

> Substitute the term number for n.

  Answer: 4, 8, ...

  b Work out the 20th term. ....

2 Write the first five terms of the sequence with the general term $10n$ ....

3 The general term of a sequence is $n + 5$

  a Write the first four terms of the sequence.

  1st term, 2nd term, 3rd term, 4th term

    $1 + 5$ $2 + 5$ $3 + 5$ $4 + 5$

  Answer: 6, ...

  b Work out the 20th term. ....

  c Describe the sequence by giving the 1st term and the common difference.

4 Find the general term of each sequence.

  a 5, 6, 7, 8, ...

  Term number   1 2 3 4 ......

  + ...

  Term   5 6 7 8 ...... n+ ...... + ...

> What do you do to the term number to get the term?

  b 12, 13, 14, 15, ...

5 Work out the first five terms of the sequence for each general term.

  a $5n + 2$ ....   **b** $2n - 2$ ....

> $5 \times \mathbf{1} + 2,$
> $5 \times \mathbf{2} + 2,$
> $5 \times \mathbf{3} + 2, ...$

6 Work out the general term of each sequence.

  a   10, 12, 14, 16, ...

      + 2 + 2 + 2

> First work out the common difference.

  + 8   2   4   6   8

        10 12 14 16 + 8

> The common difference is 2, so compare it to the multiples of 2 (called $2n$). You need to add 8 to get the sequence.

Worked example

  b 6, 8, 10, 12, ...   **c** 1, 11, 21, 31, ...

CHECK   Tick each box as your **confidence** in this topic improves.

Need extra help? Go to pages 101–102 and tick the boxes next to Q6–12 and 14. Then have a go at them once you've finished 10.1–10.5.

97

1 For each sequence in parts **a** and **b**

   i draw the next two patterns

   ii complete the table

   iii write the 1st term and the term-to-term rule.

Worked example

a

Term number	1	2	3	4	5
Number of lines	6	9			

(Guided)

b

Term number	1	2	3	4	5
Number of dots	3	8			

2 The 1st term of a sequence is 5. The term-to-term rule is 'double the previous term'.

   Write the first five terms in the sequence. ....

3 Describe each sequence by giving the 1st term and the term-to-term rule.

(Guided)

   a 1, 2, 4, 8, ...   1st term = ..., term-to-term rule: ×2

   b 32, 16, 8, 4, ...   1st term = 32,   term-to-term rule: ....

   c 81, 27, 9, 3, ...

   d 0.02, 0.2, 2, 20, ...

> In a **geometric sequence**, the term-to-term rule is 'multiply by ☐'. You find each term by multiplying the previous term in the sequence by a constant value.

4 Decide whether each sequence is arithmetic or geometric.

   a 1, 3, 9, 27, ...

   b 5, 10, 15, 20, ...

   c 1000, 100, 10, 1, ...

5 For each geometric sequence write the next two terms.

   a 500, 250, 125, ... , ...   **b** 4, 16, 64, ... , ...

   c 500, 50, 5, ... , ...   **d** 2, 10, 50, ... , ...

6 Work out the first three terms of the sequence for each general term.

   a $n^2 + 10$ ....

   b $10n^2$ ....

   c $\frac{n^2}{10}$ ....

CHECK   Tick each box as your **confidence** in this topic improves.

Need extra help? Go to pages 101–102 and tick the boxes next to Q3, 13 and 14. Then have a go at them once you've finished 10.1–10.5.

1 The length of the line segment CD is 10 units.

a Work out the length of the line segment AB.

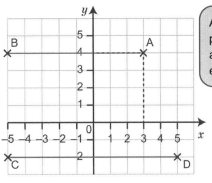

A **line segment** is part of a line. It has a beginning and an end point.

b Write the coordinates of each point.

A (3, ...)

Look at point B. Read off the coordinate from the *x*-axis and then the *y*-axis.

B ....

C ....

D ....

The *x*- and *y*-axes extend below 0, so you can plot points with negative *x*- and *y*-coordinates. The point (0, 0) is called the **origin**.

2 a On the grid from Q1, plot and label these points

E (−1, 0)   F(−2, 1)   G(0, 3)   H(1, 2)

b Join the points in alphabetical order. What shape have you made? ....

3 Work out the coordinates of the midpoint of each line segment.

a AB ....

b CD ....

c EF ....

d GH ....

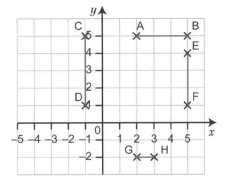

Find the point halfway between A and B. Write its coordinates.

4 Work out the midpoint of each line segment.

a I (−5, 4)   J (3, 4) ....

b K (4, 5)   L (4, −1) ....

c M (−5, 3)   N (−5, 0) ....

Plot each pair of points on the grid and join them. Then mark the midpoints.

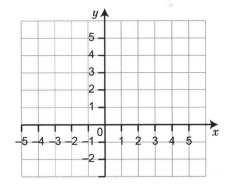

5 Find the midpoint of the line segment joining each pair of points.

a O (−4, −1)   P (−2, −3)..................... **b** Q (−1, −2)   R (0, −1) ....

c S (1, −2)   T (3, 3) .... **d** U (10, −7)   V (−5, 12) ....

Worked example

CHECK Tick each box as your **confidence** in this topic improves.

Need extra help? Go to pages 102–103 and tick the boxes next to Q15 and 21. Then have a go at them once you've finished 10.1–10.5.

10.5 Graphs

1 a Write the coordinates of four points on line A.

b What do you notice about the x-coordinates?

c Complete this statement.

The equation of line A is $x =$ ....

d Draw and label these graphs.

   i $x = -2$ **ii** $x = 4$

   iii $y = 4$ **iv** $y = -2$

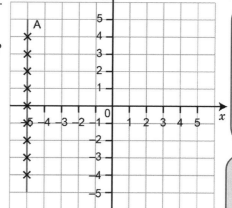

> A line on a coordinate grid is called a **graph**.
> You can describe it by giving the **equation** of the line.

> When you draw a graph it should go to the edge of the grid.

2 Look at these points.

   V (4, 3)   W (3, 6)   X (−3, 3)   Y (3, −5)   Z (3, 3)

   Which of them are on the line   **a** $x = 3$ ....   **b** $y = 3$? ....

3 a Complete the table of values for the equation $y = x$

x	0	1	2	3	4
y	0	1			

b Write down the coordinate pairs from the table.

(0, 0), ...

c Plot and label the graph of $y = x$

d Complete the table of values for the equation $y = x + 2$

x	0	1	2	3	4
y	0 + 2 = 2				

e Write down the coordinate pairs from the table. (0, 2), ...

f Plot and label the graph of $y = x + 2$

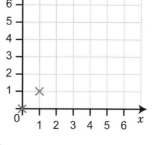

> Plot the coordinate pairs. Draw a straight line through the points and continue it to the edge of the grid.

4 a Complete the table of values for the equation $y = 2x + 2$.

x	−2	−1	0	1	2
y					

b Plot and label the graph of $y = 2x + 2$

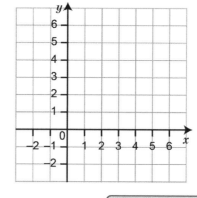

> **Worked example**
>

5 On the grid from Q1

   a plot and label the graph of $y = x$

   b plot and label the graph of $y = -x$

> In part **a**, use the points from Q3a to help you.

> In part **b**, the y-coordinate will always be equal to the x-coordinate, but with the opposite sign, for example (2, −2) or (−2, 2).

CHECK   Tick each box as your **confidence** in this topic improves.

Need extra help? Go to pages 102–103 and tick the boxes next to Q15–20. Then have a go at them once you've finished 10.1–10.5.

Sequences

☐ **1** An arithmetic sequence starts 2, 5, 8, 11, ...

    a What is the common difference? ....

    b Work out the next two terms. ....

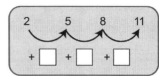

In an arithmetic sequence you add or subtract the *same* number each time.

☐ **2 a** Work out the next three terms of each sequence.

    i 25, 21, 17, 13, ..., ..., ...

    ii 12, 17, 22, 27, ..., ..., ...

    iii 8, 17, 26, 35, ..., ..., ...

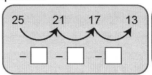

Literacy hint
Ascending numbers get bigger.
Descending numbers get smaller.

    b Is each sequence ascending or descending? **i** .... **ii** .... **iii** ....

☐ **3** Look at this sequence made of dots.

    1   2   3

    a Draw the next pattern in the sequence.

    b Complete the table.

    c Work out the number of dots in pattern number 6. ....

Pattern number	1	2	3	4	5
Number of dots	3	6			

☐ **4** The 1st term of an arithmetic sequence is 2. The common difference is 4.
Complete the table to find the first five terms of this sequence.

Term number	1st	2nd	3rd	4th	5th
Term	2	2 + 4 = 6	6 + ... = ...	..... + ... = ...	

☐ **5** Find the next three terms of each arithmetic sequence.

    a 1st term = 7   common difference = 4   2nd term = ... , 3rd term = ... , 4th term = ...

    b 1st term = 15   common difference = –3   2nd term = ... , 3rd term = ... , 4th term = ...

☐ **6** For each sequence work out   **i** the general term   **ii** the 10th term.

    a 4, 8, 12, 16, ...   **i** These are multiples of 4, so the general term is 4n.

            ii General term is 4n, so 10th term is 4 × 10 = ...

1st term: **1** × ☐ = 4
2nd term: **2** × ☐ = 8
...
10th term: **10** × ☐ = ☐

    b 10, 20, 30, 40, ...   **i** ....

            ii ....

    c 7, 14, 21, 28, ...   **i** ....

            ii ....

☐ **7** Look at the sequence in the table.

Term number	1	2	3	4	n
Term	6	7	8	9	...

n + ☐

    a What do you add to the term number each time to get the term? ....

    b Write the general term of the sequence. ....

8 Work out the general term of each sequence.

Draw a table to help you.

  a 13, 14, 15, 16, 17, ...

n − □

  b −1, 0, 1, 2, 3, ...

9 The general term (*n*th term) of a sequence is *n* + 11
Work out the first five terms.

1st term: **1** + 11 = □
2nd term: **2** + □ = □

10 The general term (*n*th term) of a sequence is 2*n* + 5. Work out the first five terms.

Guided

nth term: 2 × *n* + 5

1st term: 2 × 1 + 5 = 7

Substitute *n* = 1, *n* = 2, ..., *n* = 5 into 2*n* + 5.

7, ...

11 These two sequences have the same common difference.

Sequence A is multiples of □.

Sequence A   2, 4, 6, 8, 10, ...   Sequence B   5, 7, 9, 11, 13, ...

  a Work out the general term of sequence A. ....

  b What do you add to each term in sequence A

+ □ ⟨ 2 4 6 8 10 / 5 7 9 11 13 ⟩ + □

   to get the terms in sequence B? ....

  c Complete the general term of sequence B: 2*n* + ...

12 Work out the general term of the sequence 5, 8, 11, 14, 17, ...

13 Tick the geometric sequences.

In a geometric sequence the term-to-term rule is to multiply or divide by the same number each time.

  a 1, 2, 3, 4, ...   **b** 1, 2, 4, 8, ...

  c 7, 11, 15, 19, ...   **d** 100, 50, 25, 12.5, ...

14 For each sequence work out   **i** the next two terms in the sequence   **ii** the term-to-term rule.

Guided

  a 1   3   9   27   ....   rule: ....

For ascending sequences try + □ and × □
For descending sequences try − □ and ÷ □

      × ...... × ...... × ...... × ...... × ......

  b 2, 10, 50, 250, ... , ... rule: ....   **c** 4, 9, 14, 19, ... , ... rule: ....

  d 5, 15, 45, 135, ... , ... rule: ....   **e** 20, 18, 16, 14, ... , ... rule: ....

Graphs

15 a Plot these points.

Guided

To plot the point (−3, 2) move 3 left along the *x*-axis and 2 up the *y*-axis.

   (−3, 2), (−1, 2), (0, 2), (2, 2), (4, 2)

   Draw a line through all the points.

  b What do you notice about the *y*-coordinate of all the points?

....

  c Complete this statement.

   'The equation of the line is *y* = ... It is parallel to the ..... -axis.'

16 Write the coordinates of four points that lie on the graph of

Guided

  a *y* = −2   (5, -2), (4, -2), ...

The *y*-value is *always* −2.

  b *x* = 10   ....

The *x*-value is *always* 10.

17 a Complete the table of values for the equation $y = x + 4$.

x	0	1	2	3	4	5
y	4					

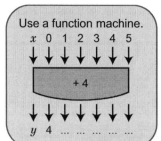

Use a function machine.

b Write each pair of coordinates from the table.

(0, 4), (1, ...), (2, ...), (3, ...), (4, ...), (5, ...)

18 a Complete the table of values for the equation $y = 4x$.

x	0	1	2	3	4
y	0				

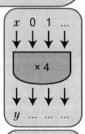

b Write each pair of coordinates from the table.

19 Complete the table of values for the equation $y = 4x - 2$.

x	0	1	2	3	4
y	-2				

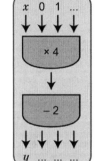

20 On the grid plot the points and join them with a straight line to draw the graph of

a $y = x + 4$, from Q17

b $y = 4x$, from Q18

c $y = 4x - 2$, from Q19

d $y = x$

e $y = -x$

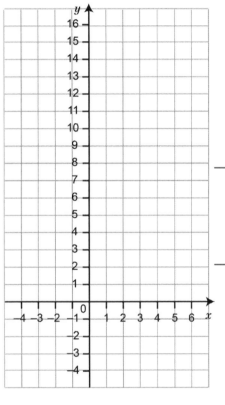

Read the equation of the graph aloud, 'y equals x'. This means that the x- and y-coordinates are the same.

Read the equation of the graph aloud, 'y equals minus x'. This means that the y-coordinate is the negative of the x-coordinate.

21 a What number is halfway between **i** 3 and 7 .... **ii** 1 and 5? ....

Add the values together and divide by 2.

b Use your answers to help you find the coordinates of the midpoint of this line segment.

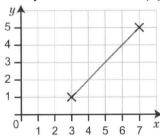

The midpoint of a line segment is the point halfway between the two ends. Find the number halfway between 1 and 12, and the number halfway between 7 and 16.

c Work out the midpoint of the line segment joining

i (1, 7) and (12, 16) .... **ii** (3, 4) and (6, 5) ....

1 Two of the corners of a square are at the points (–3, 1) and (1, 1).

  a Write down possible coordinates for

    the other two corners. ....

  b Write down two other possible coordinates

    for the two corners. ....

> Plot the two points first.

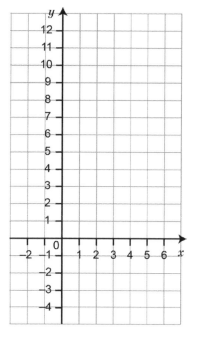

2 a Complete the table of values for the equation $y = 2x - 2$

x	–1	0	1	2	3
y	2 × -1 - 2 = -4				

  b Complete the table of values for the equation $y = 10 - x$

x	–2	0	2	4	6
y	10 - -2 = 12				

  c Plot and label the graphs of $y = 2x - 2$ and $y = 10 - x$ on the grid.

  d Write the coordinates of the point where
the two graphs **intersect**. ....

> **Literacy hint**
> **Intersect** means 'cross'.

3 Reasoning   A restaurant has trapezium shaped tables,
and 5 people can sit at each one.
When 2 tables are put together, 8 people can sit at them.

  a How many people can sit at 3 tables put together? ....

  b Complete this table of values.

Number of tables	1	2	3	4	5
Number of seats	5	8			

  c How many people can sit at 10 tables? ....

  d How many extra seats are made each time a table is added? ....

  e Billy says the general term for the number of seats for n tables put together is $5n$,

    since five people can sit at each table. Is he right? Explain your answer.

  f Work out the general term for the number of seats for n tables. ....

  g How many tables are needed for 30 people? ....

4 Reasoning   Write the equation of the line that
goes through the points

  a A, B and C ....

  b A, D and E ....

  c F, G and H. ....

  d Does the graph in part **c** go through point A?
Explain your answer.

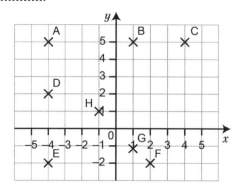

5 On the grid in Q4 plot and label these three corners of a parallelogram WXYZ.

W (1, 1), X (4, 1), Y (5, 5)

   a What are the coordinates of point Z? ....

   b Work out the coordinates of the midpoint of

      i WX ....   **ii** XY. ....

6 Reasoning The general term of a sequence is $5n + 2$

   a Which of these numbers are in the sequence? Explain your answers.

      i 7 ....

      ii 55 ....

      iii 672 ....

      iv −3 ....

   b Which number term has the value 162? ....

   c Which term is the first term greater than 400? ....

Worked example

7 Problem-solving The general term of a sequence is $-6n - 2.5$

   a Is the sequence finite or infinite? ....

   b Which term has the highest value? What is this value? ....

8 Work out the next two terms in each sequence.

   a +3 +5 +7 +9

      3, 6, 11, 18, 27, ... , ...

   b 0, $\frac{1}{3}$, 1, 2, $3\frac{1}{3}$, ... , ...

   c 2, −2, 2, −2, 2, ... , ...   **d** 2, −1, 3, −2, 4, ... , ...

9 The first two terms of a sequence are 1 and 5.
The sequence could be arithmetic *or* geometric.

   a For an arithmetic sequence starting 1, 5, …

      i write the next two terms ....

      ii work out the nth term. ....

   b For a geometric sequence starting 1, 5, …

      i write the next two terms ....

      ii describe the sequence, giving the 1st term and the term-to-term rule. ....

10 Reasoning The first four terms of a geometric sequence are 3, 9, 27, 81, …

   a Write the 5th term in the sequence. ....

   b Complete the table.

1st term	2nd term	3rd term	4th term	5th term
3	3 × 3 = 3^2	3 × 3 × 3 = 3...	.... = 3..	.... = 3...

   c Work out the 10th term of the sequence. ....

   d Write the general term of the sequence. ....

PROGRESS BAR Colour in the progress bar as you get questions correct.
Then fill in the progression chart on pages 107–109.

1 Look at this sequence.

   a Draw the next term.

   b Complete the table.

Term number	1	2	3	4	5	6
Number of dots	1	4				

2 The first five terms of a sequence are 4, 8, 12, 16, 20.

   What is the 8th term? ....

3 Work out the first four terms of an arithmetic sequence with 1st term 5 and common difference 6.

4 Is the sequence 5, 10, 20, 40, ... arithmetic or geometric? Explain your answer.

5 Work out the general term of each sequence.

   a 11, 22, 33, 44, ...

   b 11, 15, 19, 23, ...

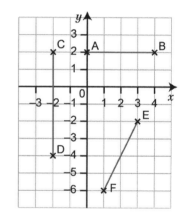

6 Calculate the midpoint of each line segment shown on the grid.

   AB ....

   CD ....

   EF ....

7 a Work out the first three terms of the sequence with nth term $2n - 4$.

   b Complete the table of values for $y = 2x - 4$.

x	−1	0	1	2	3
y					

   c On the grid from Q6 plot the graph of $y = 2x - 4$.

8 Clive sketched four graphs.
Which one represents the graph with equation $y = x$?

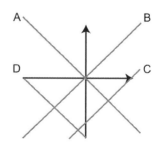

9 A geometric sequence starts 10, 100, 1000, ...

   a Write the 4th and 5th terms of the sequence. ....

   b What is the general term? ....

Progression charts

Progression is all about checking your confidence in the maths that you're learning.
- For each Unit test, tick the questions you answered correctly.
- Then rate your confidence by ticking a smiley face.

1 Analysing and displaying data

I can...	Unit 1: Unit test		
Calculate mean from a frequency table; find modal class of a continuous data set and know when to use mean, median or mode.	Q2 ☐	Q3 ☐	Q4 ☐
Use two way tables for discrete data and construct and interpret scatter graphs.	Q1 ☐	Q5 ☐	
My confidence	☹ ☐	☺ ☐	☺ ☐

2 Number skills

I can...	Unit 2: Unit test		
Find the HCF or LCM of 2 numbers less than 20 and find square and cube roots by factorising.	Q1 ☐	Q2 ☐	Q10 ☐
Calculate with positive and negative integers and estimate answers to calculations involving 2 or more operations and BIDMAS.	Q4 ☐	Q9 ☐	
Estimate square roots and give the positive and negative square root of a number.	Q5 ☐	Q6 ☐	
Divide three-digit by two-digit whole numbers.	Q3 ☐		
Work with calculations where brackets are squared or square rooted and extend calculations to cubes and cube roots.	Q7 ☐	Q8 ☐	Q11 ☐
My confidence	☹ ☐	☺ ☐	☺ ☐

3 Expressions, functions and formulae

I can...	Unit 3: Unit test		
Simplify expressions by collecting like terms.	Q8 ☐	Q9 ☐	Q10 ☐
Construct expressions from worded descriptions and substitute positive integers into expressions involving small powers.	Q5 ☐	Q6 ☐	Q13 ☐
Evaluate an expression by substituting a positive value into the expression x^2.	Q12 ☐		
Use the distributive law to take out numerical common factors.	Q14 ☐		
Multiply a single term over a bracket	Q5 ☐	Q11 ☐	
Substitute positive integers into formulae expressed in words and in symbols.	Q1 ☐	Q2 ☐	
My confidence	☹ ☐	☺ ☐	☺ ☐

4 Fractions

I can...	Unit 4: Unit test			
Simplify and compare fractions and convert between fractions, decimals and percentages.	Q1 ☐	Q7 ☐		
Multiply a fraction by an integer and divide by a fraction.	Q6 ☐	Q9 ☐		
Add, subtract or multiply fractions and calculate fractions of quantities and measurements.	Q2 ☐	Q3 ☐	Q12 ☐	
Calculate with mixed numbers and express time as a mixed number.	Q4 ☐	Q5 ☐	Q8 ☐	Q10 ☐
	Q11 ☐	Q13 ☐	Q14 ☐	
My confidence ☹ ☐ 😐 ☐ 🙂 ☐				

5 Angles and shapes

I can...	Unit 5: Unit test			
Solve simple geometrical problems, using reasoning.	Q1 ☐	Q6 ☐	Q8 ☐	Q10 ☐
Calculate angles in triangles and the interior and exterior angles of regular and irregular polygons.	Q2 ☐	Q4 ☐	Q7 ☐	Q9 ☐
Identify symmetries of 2-D shapes and classify quadrilaterals by their geometric properties.	Q3 ☐	Q5 ☐		
My confidence ☹ ☐ 😐 ☐ 🙂 ☐				

6 Decimals

I can...	Unit 6: Unit test			
Order positive and negative decimals and round numbers to two or three decimal places.	Q5 ☐	Q6 ☐	Q11 ☐	
Add, subtract, multiply and divide integers or decimals.	Q2 ☐	Q7 ☐		
Use place value to calculate the product of two decimals where original fact is given.	Q4 ☐			
Find equivalent fractions, decimals and percentages.	Q3 ☐			
Work out percentages of an amount and find the outcome of a percentage increase or decrease.	Q1 ☐	Q8 ☐	Q9 ☐	Q10 ☐
My confidence ☹ ☐ 😐 ☐ 🙂 ☐				

7 Equations

I can...	Unit 7: Unit test			
Solve simple linear and two-step linear equations with integer coefficients.	Q1 ☐	Q2 ☐	Q3 ☐	Q6 ☐
Substitute integers into formulae and use trial and improvement to find solutions to equations.	Q4 ☐	Q8 ☐		

Construct and solve equations of the form $a(x +/- b) = c(x +/- d)$	Q5 ☐
Find a positive and negative square root as a solution of an equation involving x^2.	Q7 ☐

My confidence 🙁 ☐ 😐 ☐ 🙂 ☐

8 Multiplicative reasoning

I can...	Unit 8: Unit test		
Reduce a ratio to its simplest form and simplify a ratio expressed in different units.	Q1 ☐	Q3 ☐	Q9 ☐
Convert between measures and compare ratios by changing them to the form $1{:}n$ or $n{:}1$.	Q4 ☐	Q10 ☐	Q11 ☐
Divide a quantity into 2 or more parts in a given ratio and simplify or write ratios using fractions, decimals or percentages.	Q2 ☐	Q5 ☐	Q7 ☐
Solve word problems involving ratio and proportion and use the unitary method.	Q6 ☐	Q8 ☐	Q12 ☐

My confidence 🙁 ☐ 😐 ☐ 🙂 ☐

9 Perimeter, area and volume

I can...	Unit 9: Unit test	
Use a formula to calculate the area of triangles, parallelograms and trapeziums and calculate the perimeter and area of compound shapes.	Q1 ☐	Q3 ☐
Find the surface area of cuboids and the volume of cubes, cuboids or solids made from cuboids.	Q2 ☐	Q5 ☐
Convert between area measures and convert cm^3 to ml and litres and vice versa.	Q4 ☐	Q6 ☐

My confidence 🙁 ☐ 😐 ☐ 🙂 ☐

10 Sequences and graphs

I can...	Unit 10: Unit test			
Generate terms of a linear sequence, find a term given its position in a sequence and describe the nth term in an arithmetic sequence.	Q1 ☐	Q2 ☐	Q3 ☐	Q5 ☐
Recognise geometric sequences, find their term-to-term rule and continue to the next few terms.	Q4 ☐	Q9 ☐		
Read and plot x and y co-ordinates in all four quadrants and plot and recognise graphs of $y = x$ and $y = -x$.	Q7 ☐	Q8 ☐		
Find the midpoint of a line segment.	Q6 ☐			

My confidence 🙁 ☐ 😐 ☐ 🙂 ☐

Progress with confidence

Our innovative Progression Workbooks are focussed on building your confidence in maths and let you take control of your learning.

- Chart how well you're doing against specific Learning Objectives with Progression Charts for each Unit
- Keep track of your strengths and weaknesses with Confidence Checkers at the end of each lesson and Unit
- Take control of your work and progression with loads of write-in practice

The Workbooks also offer plenty of dynamic support to help build your confidence in maths.

- Get direct access to worked example videos on your phone or tablet using the QR codes, providing crucial support for tricky questions
- Help structure your answers with guided questions and partially worked solutions
- Break down any barriers to learning with hints and key learning points for each topic

Delivering the 2014 National Curriculum

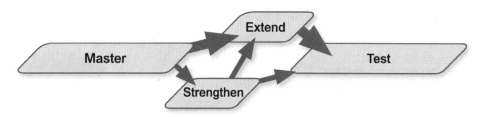

Progress with confidence with hundreds of extra practice questions for Fluency, Problem-solving and Reasoning, as well as Modelling, Finance, Real and STEM.

Other components include: Student Books, ActiveTeach Presentation, Teacher Guides and ActiveLearn online homework.

For more information visit www.pearsonschools.co.uk/ks3mathsprogress

www.pearsonschools.co.uk
myorders@pearson.com

T 0845 630 33 33
F 0845 630 77 77

ISBN 978-1-4479-7110-8

9 781447 971108